PostgreSQL Developer's Guide

Design, develop, and implement streamlined databases with PostgreSQL

Ibrar Ahmed

Asif Fayyaz

Amjad Shahzad

[PACKT] open source
PUBLISHING   community experience distilled

BIRMINGHAM - MUMBAI

PostgreSQL Developer's Guide

Copyright © 2015 Packt Publishing

First published: February 2015

Production reference: 1230215

Published by Packt Publishing Ltd.
Livery Place
35 Livery Street
Birmingham B3 2PB, UK.

ISBN 978-1-78398-902-7

www.packtpub.com

Credits

Authors
Ibrar Ahmed
Asif Fayyaz
Amjad Shahzad

Reviewers
Daniel Durante
Vinit Kumar
Jean Lazarou
Ľuboš Medovarský

Commissioning Editor
Julian Ursell

Acquisition Editors
Richard Harvey
Greg Wild

Content Development Editor
Samantha Gonsalves

Technical Editor
Gaurav Suri

Copy Editors
Shivangi Chaturvedi
Deepa Nambiar
Adithi Shetty

Project Coordinator
Sanchita Mandal

Proofreaders
Ting Baker
Simran Bhogal
Paul Hindle

Indexer
Hemangini Bari

Production Coordinator
Melwyn D'sa

Cover Work
Melwyn D'sa

About the Authors

Ibrar Ahmed has over 15 years of experience in software development. He is currently working as a software architect for a PostgreSQL-based company. He is an open source evangelist. He has contributed features such as pg_migrator (now called pg_upgrade) and Index Only Scans to PostgreSQL and has contributed to Google Chromium projects such as platform-independent FTP implementations of the Google Chrome browser, Chromium test framework enhancements, and porting of listen_socket and telnet_server to Linux. He has a lot of experience in implementing network protocols and writing Linux kernel modules. Apart from his professional life, he delivers lectures at universities and reads books.

> I would like to thank my loving parents for everything they did for me. Personal time always belongs to family, and I did this in my personal time, so thanks to my family for all the support. I would also like to thank Mr. Richard Harvey, who encouraged me to write the book, and my early age mentor, Mr. Mahmood Hussain, who helped me a lot at the start of my professional career. It has been a really great experience to work with Amjad Shahzad and Asif Fayyaz.

Asif Fayyaz is an open source technology lover and practitioner. He is currently working as a senior software quality assurance engineer at a leading PostgreSQL-based company. He has been learning and using PostgreSQL for the last 7 years. His areas of interest are exploring PostgreSQL replication solutions and software test automation solutions for desktop, web, and mobile applications. His future endeavors include joining a sports channel for set-top box automation in Python.

Apart from his professional activities, he, along with his dedicated friends, is keen to find ways that can make life easier for those who are facing the worst living conditions.

His other passions include, but are not limited to, traveling to different places, trying different cuisines, and reading books if somehow permitted by his loving family.

I would like to thank my loving parents, encouraging siblings, friends, colleagues, my caring wife, and adorable daughter for not only bearing with my busy schedule but motivating me as well to get all this done.

I would also like to thank my colleagues, Ibrar Ahmed, for his technical expertise and guidance, and Amjad Shahzad, for his constant moral and technical support.

A thumbs up to Packt Publishing and notably to Richard, Gregory, Azhar, and Samantha. You folks were great mentors and got the best out of us. Undoubtedly a great experience!

Amjad Shahzad has been working in the open source software industry for the last 10 years. He is currently working as a senior quality assurance engineer at a leading PostgreSQL-based company, which is the only worldwide provider of enterprise-class products and services based on PostgreSQL. Amjad's core expertise lies in the areas of pg_upgrade, slony and streaming replication, Cloud database, and database partitioning. His future endeavors include exploring PostgreSQL replication solutions.

Apart from his professional activities, he is also involved in doing social activities that involve helping people stand on their feet. In his free time, he likes to explore nature by doing outdoor activities, including hiking, trekking, and nature photography.

I would like to say a special thank you to my parents, who have been my source of inspiration since the start of my career. I would also like to thank my wife for putting up with my late night writing sessions. I would also like to thank Ibrar Ahmed, without whom this book would not have been possible.

Finally, I want to thank the Packt Publishing staff, which includes Richard, Gregory, Azhar, and Samantha for their continuous support.

About the Reviewers

Daniel Durante is an avid coffee drinker, motorcyclist, and rugby player. He has been programming since he was 12 years old. He has been mostly involved with web development from PHP-to-Golang while using PostgreSQL as his main choice of data storage.

He has worked on text-based browser games that have reached over 1,000,000 players, created bin-packing software for CNC machines, and helped contribute to one of the oldest ORMs of Node.js.

> I would like to thank my parents, my brother, and friends who've all put up with my insanity sitting in front of a computer day in and day out. I would not have been here today if it wasn't for their patience, guidance, and love.

Vinit Kumar is an autodidact engineer who cares about writing beautiful code that scales well.

He has a good amount of experience in building social networks, multi-tenant systems, content management systems, and embedded website infrastructure. His main areas of interest are building performant systems, functional programming, and solving problems that really matter.

Vinit is an active member of the free and open source software community and has contributed to many projects, including Node.js, Python, and Django.

Prior to his current position, he worked as an application development consultant and wrote applications for clients all over the world.

Vinit is a full-time developer who builds Socialschools (`http://socialschools.nl`), which is a safe and secure social network for schools.

These days, he writes a lot of Django code along with frontend work on backbone layers. He also works closely with the mobile team (iOS and Android) to ensure that they get proper APIs and documentation support to get their job done.

He also helps his team write good maintainable code by doing code reviews and following good practices such as Git, documentation, and tooling.

I would like to thank my family and fiance for having enough patience to allow me to spend time on reviewing this book. Also, I would like to thank the folks at Packt Publishing for being in constant touch during the course of review.

Jean Lazarou started spending time with computers at the age of 15.

He has worked in various sectors, such as the medical industry, the manufacturing industry, university education, and the multimedia world.

He mainly uses Basic, C/C++, Java, and Ruby to develop fat clients, web applications, frameworks, tools, and compilers, often involving databases.

He has published his personal works on GitHub and some technical articles on his blog.

Ľuboš Medovarský is an entrepreneur and open source C/C++, Pascal, Python, and Java software developer with experience in GNU/Linux and OpenBSD administration, configuration management, monitoring, networking, firewalls, and embedded systems.

Discontented with today's fragmented and broken state of home automation and the Internet of Things, he has developed hardware and software for the Whistler automation smart house project, which aims to disrupt the market with platform unification, privacy by design, device autonomy, built-in artificial intelligence, and security – all in open source packages and affordable for the masses. Accelera Networks s.r.o., the company he founded in 2006, develops custom software and hardware applications as well as provides IT management services. Previously, he was employed with Alcatel, Hewlett-Packard, AT&T, Erste Group, and a handful of smaller companies. When he's not at work, the trekkie inside him dreams of space colonization and the technological advancement of humanity. His favorite outdoor activities include biking and flying in a glider.

I would like to thank my wife, Izabela, and daughter, Zoja, for their patience and understanding and for the joy of life in their proximity.

www.PacktPub.com

Support files, eBooks, discount offers, and more

For support files and downloads related to your book, please visit www.PacktPub.com.

Did you know that Packt offers eBook versions of every book published, with PDF and ePub files available? You can upgrade to the eBook version at www.PacktPub.com and as a print book customer, you are entitled to a discount on the eBook copy. Get in touch with us at service@packtpub.com for more details.

At www.PacktPub.com, you can also read a collection of free technical articles, sign up for a range of free newsletters and receive exclusive discounts and offers on Packt books and eBooks.

https://www2.packtpub.com/books/subscription/packtlib

Do you need instant solutions to your IT questions? PacktLib is Packt's online digital book library. Here, you can search, access, and read Packt's entire library of books.

Why subscribe?

- Fully searchable across every book published by Packt
- Copy and paste, print, and bookmark content
- On demand and accessible via a web browser

Free access for Packt account holders

If you have an account with Packt at www.PacktPub.com, you can use this to access PacktLib today and view 9 entirely free books. Simply use your login credentials for immediate access.

Table of Contents

Preface

PostgreSQL is the world's most advanced community-driven open source database. The first open source version of PostgreSQL was released on 1st August 1996, an combined effort between Bruce Momjian and Vadim B. Mikheev. Since then, major releases have come annually, and all releases are available under its free and open source software PostgreSQL license similar to the BSD and MIT licenses. Modern technologies are emerging with new features on a regular basis, and PostgreSQL is one of the fantastic examples of this happening, adding more robust features to cope with the changing trends of technology. Developer and database administrators love to use PostgreSQL because of its reliability, scalability, and continuous support from the open source community.

PostgreSQL Developer's Guide is for database developers fascinated with learning and understanding PostgreSQL from its release. A basic awareness of database concepts is required to understand all of the PostgreSQL technical terms. As a result, by reading this guide, you, as a reader, will be able to understand how applications can be programmed with PostgreSQL, along with the core development concepts. By the end of this book, you will have a solid base in the fundamental development concepts and be able to develop database applications by leveraging the core programming functionality of PostgreSQL.

The main objective of this book is to teach you in programming database applications and custom programmatic functions. It is a practical tutorial book with an emphasis to provide authentic world examples of how applications can be programmed with PostgreSQL and grips on core development concepts and functions. By the end of this book, we will show you how to write custom programming functions, which extends the PostgreSQL database beyond its core capabilities. We wish you the best of luck on your quest of seeking knowledge of PostgreSQL, where we hope that at the end of this book, you will feel like you deserve a pat on the back for your efforts in acquiring some hands-on expertise with PostgreSQL.

What this book covers

Chapter 1, Getting Started with PostgreSQL, explains the birth, present, and future along with the evolution of PostgreSQL in terms of its features, maintainability, and its immensely huge global following. This chapter will explain the concepts of DDL (Data Description Language) and DML (Data Manipulation Language), and explain how to write DDL and DML statements.

Chapter 2, The Procedural Language, encompasses the diversified features of PL/pgSQL, native support for four languages, and extensibility for others. We will skim through the description of PL/pgSQL by explaining its structure, declarations, and verbal expressions. This chapter will shed light on using native support and utilization examples of other procedural languages such as PL/Python, PL/Tcl, and PL/Perl.

Chapter 3, Working with Indexes, is all about indexes, so expect to see a discussion of the fundamental concepts of indexes, such as the kinds of indexes PostgreSQL supports and the syntax to create them. The main story of this chapter is where to utilize what kind of index and which condition it is best suited for. You can then build different kinds of indexes in the warehouse database to explicate the practical use of indexes.

Chapter 4, Triggers, Rules, and Views, consists of three sections: triggers, rules, and views. The first section of this chapter will explain what a trigger is and how to create triggers in PostgreSQL. The second part will deal with PostgreSQL rules. There will be a focus on how the rules work by explaining their call, input, and the results. The final third part will revolve around views and why they are important in database design.

Chapter 5, Window Functions, discusses the power and concepts of window functions in conjunction with aggregate functions. We will also cover the scope, structure, and usage of window functions with examples. Another objective will be to acquire a crystal clear understanding of the core of window functions and the data that is processed with the help of frame, OVER, PARTITION BY, and ORDER BY clauses. This chapter will also discuss the available built-in window functions, along with custom ones.

Chapter 6, Partitioning, deals with table partitioning. Table partitioning in PostgreSQL is implemented through table inheritance. In this section, there will be a brief overview of partition in order to improve the performance of queries before moving on to its implementation in PostgreSQL. The chapter also covers the list (that utilizes key values) and range (that utilizes key columns) partitions.

Chapter 7, Query Optimization, is about query analysis and optimization. Queries can be optimized utilizing indexes and hints and manipulating planner parameters. As a reader, you will find this chapter very useful in utilizing and optimizing your queries.

Chapter 8, Dealing with Large Objects, is about the handling of Large Objects (LO) as there is a need to store large objects such as audio and video files. PostgreSQL has support to manipulate these objects. The handling of sizably huge objects is consummately different from the other objects such as text, varchar, and int. This chapter will explain why we need to store Large Objects (LO) and how PostgreSQL implements LO storage.

Chapter 9, Communicating with PostgreSQL Using LibPQ, explains how to write C programs and connect and execute queries in the C language using libpq, which is a PostgreSQL client library to communicate with the PostgreSQL server. In this chapter, we will grip on the different ways of communication by utilizing libpq and the utilization of all libpq functions. To extend our story of the warehouse database, we will write a program to manipulate the data from the database.

Chapter 10, Embedded SQL in C – ECPG, covers all the syntax and utilization of Embedded SQL to manipulate the data inside this code. Other than libpq, there is an alternative to communicate in C code to a PostgreSQL server called ECPG. Additionally, there will be coverage of how to compile the ECPG program, and we will discuss the command-line options of the ECPG binary.

Chapter 11, Foreign Data Wrapper, covers how to explain the building blocks of the foreign data wrapper and discusses how to utilize postgres_fdw and file_fdw to manipulate foreign data. PostgreSQL introduces an incipient feature called the foreign data wrapper. It's a template to write the module to access foreign data. This is rigorously based in SQL/MED standards (SQL Management of External Data). There are only two community maintained wrappers, postgres_fdw and file_fdw, along with many externally maintained foreign data wrappers.

Chapter 12, Extensions, covers how to install and use available extensions in PostgreSQL. PostgreSQL has features to install the loadable modules called extensions. Instead of creating a bunch of objects by running SQL queries, an extension, which is a collection of objects, can be created and dropped using a single command. The main advantage of an extension is maintainability. There are several extensions available.

What you need for this book

To get the most out of this book along with practical, hands-on experience, you should practice the examples described. For this, you'll need the following:

- PostgreSQL installed through the installer, which is available at
  http://www.postgresql.org/download/

- A basic text editor such as vim, gedit, or kate

- An OS Command-Line Interface (CLI) to run PostgreSQL binaries, for example, psql, postmaster, or pg_ctl

Who this book is for

This book is for database developers who are interested in learning and understanding PostgreSQL from scratch. Though you will need to know the basic database concepts in order to understand the technical terms used throughout this book, PostgreSQL is an open source and growing database community at, so having a firm grasp on this will definitely increase your confidence in the domain of open source databases.

You will be able to understand how applications can be programmed with PostgreSQL, along with understanding the core development concepts. All the examples will cover the functionality and syntax that is in compliance with the latest versions of PostgreSQL, 9.3 and 9.4.

Conventions

In this book, you will find a number of styles of text that distinguish between different kinds of information. Here are some examples of these styles, and an explanation of their meaning.

Code words in text, database table names, folder names, filenames, file extensions, pathnames, dummy URLs, user input, and Twitter handles are shown as follows: "With the ALTER TABLE command, we can add, remove, or rename table columns."

A block of code is set as follows:

```
warehouse_db=# CREATE TABLE item
  (
  item_unique INTEGER PRIMARY KEY,
  item_name TEXT,
  item_price NUMERIC,
  item_data TEXT
  );
```

When we wish to draw your attention to a particular part of a code block, the relevant lines or items are set in bold:

```
warehouse_db=# CREATE OR REPLACE FUNCTION getRecords()
RETURNS INTEGER AS $$
DECLARE
  total INTEGER;
BEGIN
  SELECT COUNT(*) INTO total FROM warehouse_tbl;
  IF (total > 0) THEN
    RETURN total;
  ELSE
    RAISE NOTICE 'table is empty';
  END IF;
END;
$$ LANGUAGE plpgsql;
```

Any command-line input or output is written as follows:

```
$ createlang plpgsql warehouse_db -U postgres
```

New terms and **important words** are shown in bold. Words that you see on the screen, in menus or dialog boxes for example, appear in the text like this: "The team added core object-oriented features in Ingres and named the new version **PostgreSQL**."

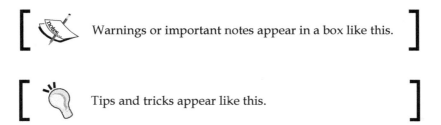

Warnings or important notes appear in a box like this.

Tips and tricks appear like this.

Reader feedback

Feedback from our readers is always welcome. Let us know what you think about this book—what you liked or may have disliked. Reader feedback is important for us to develop titles that you really get the most out of.

To send us general feedback, simply send an e-mail to feedback@packtpub.com, and mention the book title via the subject of your message.

If there is a topic that you have expertise in and you are interested in either writing or contributing to a book, see our author guide on www.packtpub.com/authors.

Customer support

Now that you are the proud owner of a Packt book, we have a number of things to help you to get the most from your purchase.

Downloading the example code

You can download the example code files for all Packt books you have purchased from your account at http://www.packtpub.com. If you purchased this book elsewhere, you can visit http://www.packtpub.com/support and register to have the files e-mailed directly to you.

Errata

Although we have taken every care to ensure the accuracy of our content, mistakes do happen. If you find a mistake in one of our books—maybe a mistake in the text or the code—we would be grateful if you would report this to us. By doing so, you can save other readers from frustration and help us improve subsequent versions of this book. If you find any errata, please report them by visiting http://www.packtpub.com/submit-errata, selecting your book, clicking on the **errata submission form** link, and entering the details of your errata. Once your errata are verified, your submission will be accepted and the errata will be uploaded on our website, or added to any list of existing errata, under the Errata section of that title. Any existing errata can be viewed by selecting your title from http://www.packtpub.com/support.

Piracy

Piracy of copyright material on the Internet is an ongoing problem across all media. At Packt, we take the protection of our copyright and licenses very seriously. If you come across any illegal copies of our works, in any form, on the Internet, please provide us with the location address or website name immediately so that we can pursue a remedy.

Please contact us at copyright@packtpub.com with a link to the suspected pirated material.

We appreciate your help in protecting our authors, and our ability to bring you valuable content.

Questions

You can contact us at questions@packtpub.com if you are having a problem with any aspect of the book, and we will do our best to address it.

1
Getting Started with PostgreSQL

Before starting our journey with SQL, allow me to quickly go through the history of PostgreSQL. It all starts from the University of California, Berkeley, in the late 1970s with the aim of developing a relational database possessing object-oriented features. They named it **Ingres**. Later on, around the mid 1980s, a team of core developers led by Michael Stonebraker from the University of California started work on Ingres. The team added core object-oriented features in Ingres and named the new version **PostgreSQL**.

This team was attached to the development of PostgreSQL for around 8 years. During this time, they introduced object-oriented concepts, procedures, rules, indexes, and types. In 1994, Andrew Yu and Jolly Chen replaced the Ingres-based query language with the SQL query language. After this change, in 1995, PostgreSQL was renamed Postgres95. In 1996, after entering the open source world, Postgres95 went through multiple changes and new features such as **Multi Version Concurrency Control (MVCC)**, and built-in types were added. Over a period of time, following the addition of new features and with the devoted work of developers, Postgres95 achieved consistency and uniformity in code. They finally renamed Postgres95 to PostgreSQL.

PostgreSQL is widely considered to be one of the most stable database servers available today, with multiple features that include:

- A wide range of built-in types
- MVCC
- New SQL enhancements, including foreign keys, primary keys, and constraints
- Open source code, maintained by a team of developers

- Trigger and procedure support with multiple procedural languages
- Extensibility in the sense of adding new data types and the client language

From the early releases of PostgreSQL (from version 6.0 that is), many changes have been made, with each new major version adding new and more advanced features. The current version is PostgreSQL 9.4 and is available from several sources and in various binary formats.

 We will be using PostgreSQL 9.4 throughout this book. So, let's download and install it so that we can start our remarkable journey in this book.

In this chapter, you will learn about the following topics:

- Writing queries using `psql`
- Creating, altering, and truncating a table
- Inserting, updating, and deleting data
- PostgreSQL-supported data types
- PostgreSQL-supported operators and usage
- Constraints and privileges in PostgreSQL

Writing queries using psql

Before proceeding, allow me to explain to you that throughout this book, we will use a warehouse database called `warehouse_db`. In this section, I will show you how you can create such a database, providing you with sample code for assistance. You will need to do the following:

1. We are assuming here that you have successfully installed PostgreSQL and faced no issues. Now, you will need to connect with the default database that is created by the PostgreSQL installer. To do this, navigate to the default path of installation, which is `/opt/PostgreSQL/9.4/bin` from your command line, and execute the following command that will prompt for a `postgres` user password that you provided during the installation:

```
/opt/PostgreSQL/9.4/bin$./psql -U postgres
Password for user postgres:
```

2. Using the following command, you can log in to the default database with the user `postgres` and you will be able to see the following on your command line:

```
psql (9.4beta1)
Type "help" for help
postgres=#
```

3. You can then create a new database called `warehouse_db` using the following statement in the terminal:

```
postgres=# CREATE DATABASE warehouse_db;
```

4. You can then connect with the `warehouse_db` database using the following command:

```
postgres=# \c warehouse_db
```

5. You are now connected to the `warehouse_db` database as the user `postgres`, and you will have the following `warehouse_db` shell:

```
warehouse_db=#
```

Let's summarize what we have achieved so far. We are now able to connect with the default database `postgres` and created a `warehouse_db` database successfully. It's now time to actually write queries using `psql` and perform some **Data Definition Language (DDL)** and **Data Manipulation Language (DML)** operations, which we will cover in the following sections.

In PostgreSQL, we can have multiple databases. Inside the databases, we can have multiple extensions and schemas. Inside each schema, we can have database objects such as tables, views, sequences, procedures, and functions.

We are first going to create a schema named `record` and then we will create some tables in this schema. To create a schema named `record` in the `warehouse_db` database, use the following statement:

```
warehouse_db=# CREATE SCHEMA record;
```

Creating, altering, and truncating a table

In this section, we will learn about creating a table, altering the table definition, and truncating the table.

Creating tables

Now, let's perform some DDL operations starting with creating tables. To create a table named `warehouse_tbl`, execute the following statements:

```
warehouse_db=# CREATE TABLE warehouse_tbl
  (
warehouse_id INTEGER NOT NULL,
warehouse_name TEXT NOT NULL,
year_created INTEGER,
street_address TEXT,
city CHARACTER VARYING(100),
state CHARACTER VARYING(2),
zip CHARACTER VARYING(10),
CONSTRAINT "PRIM_KEY" PRIMARY KEY (warehouse_id)
  );
```

The preceding statements created the table `warehouse_tbl` that has the primary key `warehouse_id`. Now, as you are familiar with the table creation syntax, let's create a sequence and use that in a table. You can create the `hist_id_seq` sequence using the following statement:

```
warehouse_db=# CREATE SEQUENCE hist_id_seq;
```

The preceding `CREATE SEQUENCE` command creates a new sequence number generator. This involves creating and initializing a new special single-row table with the name `hist_id_seq`. The user issuing the command will own the generator. You can now create the table that implements the `hist_id_seq` sequence using the following statement:

```
warehouse_db=# CREATE TABLE history
  (
history_id INTEGER NOT NULL DEFAULT nextval('hist_id_seq'),
date TIMESTAMP WITHOUT TIME ZONE,
amount INTEGER,
data TEXT,
customer_id INTEGER,
warehouse_id INTEGER,
CONSTRAINT "PRM_KEY" PRIMARY KEY (history_id),
CONSTRAINT "FORN_KEY"
FOREIGN KEY (warehouse_id)
REFERENCES warehouse_tbl(warehouse_id)
  );
```

The preceding query will create a `history` table in the `warehouse_db` database, and the `history_id` column uses the sequence as the default input value.

In this section, we successfully learned how to create a table and also learned how to use a sequence inside the table creation syntax.

Downloading the example code

You can download the example code files for all Packt books you have purchased from your account at http://www.packtpub.com. If you purchased this book elsewhere, you can visit http://www.packtpub.com/support and register to have the files e-mailed directly to you.

Altering tables

Now that we have learned how to create multiple tables, we can practice some `ALTER TABLE` commands by following this section. With the `ALTER TABLE` command, we can add, remove, or rename table columns.

Firstly, with the help of the following example, we will be able to add the `phone_no` column in the previously created table `warehouse_tbl`:

```
warehouse_db=# ALTER TABLE warehouse_tbl
   ADD COLUMN phone_no INTEGER;
```

We can then verify that a column is added in the table by describing the table as follows:

```
warehouse_db=# \d warehouse_tbl
              Table "public.warehouse_tbl"
     Column      |          Type           | Modifiers
-----------------+-------------------------+-----------
 warehouse_id    | integer                 | not null
 warehouse_name  | text                    | not null
 year_created    | integer                 |
 street_address  | text                    |
 city            | character varying(100)  |
 state           | character varying(2)    |
 zip             | character varying(10)   |
 phone_no        | integer                 |
Indexes:
   "PRIM_KEY" PRIMARY KEY, btree (warehouse_id)
Referenced by:
```

```
    TABLE "history" CONSTRAINT "FORN_KEY"FOREIGN KEY
    (warehouse_id) REFERENCES warehouse_tbl(warehouse_id) TABLE
    "history" CONSTRAINT "FORN_KEY" FOREIGN KEY (warehouse_id)
    REFERENCES warehouse_tbl(warehouse_id)
```

To drop a column from a table, we can use the following statement:

```
warehouse_db=# ALTER TABLE warehouse_tbl
    DROP COLUMN phone_no;
```

We can then finally verify that the column has been removed from the table by describing the table again as follows:

```
warehouse_db=# \d warehouse_tbl
            Table "public.warehouse_tbl"
     Column      |          Type          | Modifiers
-----------------+------------------------+-----------
 warehouse_id    | integer                | not null
 warehouse_name  | text                   | not null
 year_created    | integer                |
 street_address  | text                   |
 city            | character varying(100) |
 state           | character varying(2)   |
 zip             | character varying(10)  |
Indexes:
    "PRIM_KEY" PRIMARY KEY, btree (warehouse_id)
Referenced by:
    TABLE "history" CONSTRAINT "FORN_KEY" FOREIGN KEY
    (warehouse_id) REFERENCES warehouse_tbl(warehouse_id) TABLE
    "history" CONSTRAINT "FORN_KEY" FOREIGN KEY (warehouse_id)
    REFERENCES warehouse_tbl(warehouse_id)
```

Truncating tables

The TRUNCATE command is used to remove all rows from a table without providing any criteria. In the case of the DELETE command, the user has to provide the delete criteria using the WHERE clause. To truncate data from the table, we can use the following statement:

```
warehouse_db=# TRUNCATE TABLE warehouse_tbl;
```

We can then verify that the warehouse_tbl table has been truncated by performing a SELECT COUNT(*) query on it using the following statement:

```
warehouse_db=# SELECT COUNT(*) FROM warehouse_tbl;
 count
-------
     0
(1 row)
```

Inserting, updating, and deleting data from tables

In this section, we will play around with data and learn how to insert, update, and delete data from a table.

Inserting data

So far, we have learned how to create and alter a table. Now it's time to play around with some data. Let's start by inserting records in the `warehouse_tbl` table using the following command snippet:

```
warehouse_db=# INSERT INTO warehouse_tbl
  (
  warehouse_id,
  warehouse_name,
  year_created,
  street_address,
  city,
  state,
  zip
  )
VALUES
  (
  1,
  'Mark Corp',
  2009,
  '207-F Main Service Road East',
  'New London',
  'CT',
  4321
  );
```

We can then verify that the record has been inserted by performing a `SELECT` query on the `warehouse_tbl` table as follows:

```
warehouse_db=# SELECT warehouse_id, warehouse_name, street_address
               FROM warehouse_tbl;
 warehouse_id | warehouse_name |         street_address
--------------+----------------+------------------------------
            1 | Mark Corp      | 207-F Main Service Road  East
(1 row)
```

Updating data

Once we have inserted data in our table, we should know how to update it. This can be done using the following statement:

```
warehouse_db=# UPDATE warehouse_tbl
  SET year_created=2010
  WHERE year_created=2009;
```

To verify that a record is updated, let's perform a SELECT query on the warehouse_tbl table as follows:

```
warehouse_db=# SELECT warehouse_id, year_created FROM
               warehouse_tbl;
 warehouse_id | year_created
--------------+--------------
            1 |         2010
(1 row)
```

Deleting data

To delete data from a table, we can use the DELETE command. Let's add a few records to the table and then later on delete data on the basis of certain conditions:

```
warehouse_db=# INSERT INTO warehouse_tbl
  (
  warehouse_id,
  warehouse_name,
  year_created,
  street_address,
  city,
  state,
  zip
  )
VALUES
  (
  2,
  'Bill & Co',
  2014,
  'Lilly Road',
  'New London',
  'CT',
  4321
  );
warehouse_db=# INSERT INTO warehouse_tbl
```

```
    (
    warehouse_id,
    warehouse_name,
    year_created,
    street_address,
    city,
    state,
    zip
    )
VALUES
    (
    3,
    'West point',
    2013,
    'Down Town',
    'New London',
    'CT',
    4321
    );
```

We can then delete data from the `warehouse.tbl` table, where `warehouse_name` is `Bill & Co`, by executing the following statement:

```
warehouse_db=# DELETE FROM warehouse_tbl
    WHERE warehouse_name='Bill & Co';
```

To verify that a record has been deleted, we will execute the following SELECT query:

```
warehouse_db=# SELECT warehouse_id, warehouse_name
  FROM warehouse_tbl
  WHERE warehouse_name='Bill & Co';
 warehouse_id | warehouse_name
--------------+----------------
(0 rows)
```

 The DELETE command is used to drop a row from a table, whereas the DROP command is used to drop a complete table. The TRUNCATE command is used to empty the whole table.

PostgreSQL's supported data types

PostgreSQL is very vast when it comes to supporting different data types. Apart from existing data types, a user can add new data types in PostgreSQL. In order to add new data types, a user can use the CREATE TYPE command. The following list shows a number of built-in data types that are supported by PostgreSQL.

Let's go through all the supported data types one by one:

- bigint: This is a signed 8-byte integer, and it is represented as int8.
- bigserial: This is an auto incrementing 8-byte integer represented by the serial8 keyword.
- bit [(n)]: This is a fixed length bit string and is represented by the bit keyword.
- bit varying [(n)]: This is a variable length bit string and is represented by the varbit keyword.
- boolean: This is a logical Boolean expression and has the true or false value. It is represented by the bool keyword.
- box: This is a rectangular box on a plane and is represented by the box keyword.
- bytea: This is binary data stored in the form of a byte array and is represented by the bytea keyword.
- character [(n)]: This is a fixed length character string, and it is represented by the char[(n)] keyword, where n represents the length of the string.
- character varying[(n)]: This is a variable length character string, which is represented by the varchar[(n)] keyword.
- cidr: This is used to store the IPv4 and IPv6 network addresses. It is represented by the cidr keyword.
- circle: This is a circle on a plane, and it is represented by the circle keyword.
- date: This is a calendar date, which includes the year, month, and day.
- double Precision: This is a floating-point number of 8 bytes. It is represented by the float8 keyword.
- inet: This is used to store the IPv4 or IPv6 host addresses. The essential difference between the inet and cidr data types is that inet accepts values with nonzero bits to the right of the net mask, whereas cidr does not.
- integer: This is a signed 4-byte integer. It is represented by the int and int4 keywords.

- `interval [fields] [(p)]`: This is used to represent the time span.
- `json`: This is used to store the textual JSON data. Such data can also be stored as text, but the JSON data types have the advantage of enforcing that each stored value is valid according to the JSON rules. There are also assorted JSON-specific functions and operators available for data stored in these data types.
- `jsonb`: This is used to store binary JSON data.
- `line`: This is used to represent the infinite line in a plane.
- `lseg`: This is used to store data of a line segment on a plane.
- `macaddr`: This is used to store MAC addresses.
- `money`: This data type is used to store the currency amount.
- `numeric [(p,s)]`: This is used to store a numeric of selectable precision. It is represented by the `decimal [(p,s)]` keyword. The `s` parameter is used to represent the scale. The scale of a numeric is the count of decimal digits in the fractional part, to the right of the decimal point. The `p` parameter is used to represent precision. The precision of a numeric is the total count of significant digits in the whole number, that is, the number of digits to both sides of the decimal point. So, the number 23.5141 has a precision of 6 and a scale of 4.
- `path`: This is used to store a geomantic path on a plane.
- `pg_lsn`: This is used to store a PostgreSQL log sequence number.
- `points`: This is used to store a geometric point on a plane.
- `polygon`: This is used to store a closed geometric path on a plane.
- `real`: This is used to store a single precision, floating-point number of 4 bytes. It is represented by the `float4` keyword.
- `smallint`: This is used to store a signed 2-byte integer. It is represented by the `int2` keyword.
- `smallserial`: This is used to store an auto incrementing 2-byte integer. It is represented by the `serial2` keyword.
- `serial`: This is used to store an auto incrementing 4-byte integer. It is represented by the `serial4` keyword.
- `text`: This data type is used to store a variable length character string.
- `time [(p)] [without time zone]`: This is used to store the time of the day without a time zone.
- `time [(p)] with time zone`: This is used to store the time of the day with a time zone.

- `timestamp [(p)] [without time zone]`: This is used to store the date and time without a time zone.
- `timestamp [(p)] with time zone`: This is used to store date and time with a time zone.
- `time`, `timestamp`, and `interval`: These data types accept an optional precision value p that specifies the number of fractional digits retained in the seconds field. By default, there is no explicit bound on precision. The allowed range of p is from 0 to 6 for the timestamp and interval types.
- `Tsquery`: This is used to store a text search query.
- `tsvector`: This is used to store a text search document.
- `txid_snapshot`: This is used to store the user-level transaction ID snapshots.
- `uuid`: This is used to store universally unique identifiers.
- `xml`: This data type is served as storage for XML data.

PostgreSQL's operators and usage

As PostgreSQL has multiple operators, we will explain all of them in detail in this section.

Logical operators

Logical operators are available in PostgreSQL, and these are:

- AND
- OR
- NOT

In PostgreSQL, the values of true, false, and null are used as the valued logic system. For more detail, see the following truth table that shows how data types a and b can result in different values when combined with the different AND and OR logical operators:

a	b	a AND b	a OR b
TRUE	TRUE	TRUE	TRUE
TRUE	FALSE	FALSE	TRUE
TRUE	NULL	NULL	TRUE
FALSE	FALSE	FALSE	FALSE
FALSE	NULL	FALSE	NULL
NULL	NULL	NULL	NULL

You can then see from the following truth table how data type a can result in a different value when used with the NOT logical operator:

a	NOT a
TRUE	FALSE
FALSE	TRUE
NULL	NULL

Comparison operators

In PostgreSQL, we have the following comparison operators, as shown in the following table:

Operator	Description
<	Less than
>	Greater than
<=	Less than or equal to
>=	Greater than or equal to
=	Equal
<> or !=	Not equal

Mathematical operators

PostgreSQL also provides you with the following mathematical operators, as you can see in the following table:

Operator	Description
+	Addition
-	Subtraction
*	Multiplication
/	Division
%	Modulo (Remainder)
^	Exponentiation
|/	Square root
||/	Cube root
!	Factorial
!!	Factorial (prefix operator)

Operator	Description
@	Absolute value
&	Bitwise AND
|	Bitwise OR
#	Bitwise XOR
~	Bitwise NOT
<<	Bitwise shift left
>>	Bitwise shift right

Apart from the logical, comparison, and mathematical operators, PostgreSQL also has operators for strings, binary strings, bit strings, date/time, geometric, network address, and text search. Details of these operators are beyond the scope of this book and can be studied in more detail in the PostgreSQL documentation available at `http://www.postgresql.org/docs/9.4/static/functions-string.html`.

Constraints in PostgreSQL

PostgreSQL offers support for constraints and has coverage of multiple-level constraints. Constraints are used to enforce rules on data insertion in tables. Only data that complies with the constraint rules is allowed to be added to the table. The constraints present in PostgreSQL are:

- Unique constraints
- Not-null constraints
- Exclusion constrains
- Primary key constraints
- Foreign key constraints
- Check constraints

We will explain all of these constraints one by one with supportive examples. Let's start with the unique constraints.

Unique constraints

A **unique constraint** is a constraint that at the time of an insertion operation makes sure that data present in a column (or a group of columns) is unique with regard to all rows already present in the table. Let's create a few tables using unique constraints in the following manner:

```
warehouse_db=# CREATE TABLE tools
  (
  tool_id INTEGER UNIQUE,
  tool_name TEXT,
  tool_class NUMERIC
  );
```

Alternatively, the same constraint can be declared at the end of all columns. For instance, this can look like the following:

```
warehouse_db=# CREATE TABLE tools
  (
  tool_id INTEGER,
  tool_name TEXT,
  tool_class NUMERIC,
  UNIQUE (tool_id)
  );
```

When defining the unique constraints for a group of columns, all columns must be listed separately using commas. Consider the following example:

```
warehouse_db=# CREATE TABLE cards
  (
  card_id INTEGER,
  owner_number INTEGER,
  owner_name TEXT,
  UNIQUE (card_id, owner_number)
  );
```

The preceding query will create the cards table with a unique constraint implemented on the card_id and owner_number columns. Note that the unique constraint is not applicable on null values. This means that in the cards table, two records can have the same record if they have card_id and owner_number as null.

Not-null constraints

A **not-null constraint** makes sure that a column must have some values and a value is not left as null. Drop the previously created tools table and create the tools table again using this constraint using the following example:

```
warehouse_db=# CREATE TABLE tools
  (
  tool_id INTEGER NOT NULL,
  tool_name TEXT,
  tool_class NUMERIC
  );
```

The preceding query will create a table with a not-null constraint on the `tool_id` column. We can apply the not-null constraint on as many columns as we can. Consider the following example:

```
warehouse_db=# CREATE TABLE tools
  (
  tool_id INTEGER NOT NULL,
  tool_name TEXT NOT NULL,
  tool_class NUMERIC
  );
```

The preceding query will create the `tools` table with not-null constraints on `tool_id` and `tool_name`.

Exclusion constraints

An **exclusion constraint** is used when comparing two rows on nominative columns or expressions using the nominative operators. The result of the comparison will be false or null. Consider the following example in which the conflicting tuple is given the AND operation together:

```
warehouse_db=# CREATE TABLE movies
  (
  Title TEXT,
  Copies INTEGER
  );
```

Using the ALTER TABLE command, we get the following:

```
warehouse_db=# ALTER TABLE movies
  ADD EXCLUDE (title WITH=, copies WITH=);
```

We will create an exclusion constraint above the ALTER TABLE command. The conditions for a conflicting tuple are AND together. Now, in order for two records to conflict, we'll use the following:

```
record1.title = record2.title AND record1.copies = record2.copies.
```

Primary key constraints

In PostgreSQL, we have support for **primary key constraints**, which is actually a combination of not-null constraints and unique constraints, which means that for a column to fulfill the primary key constraints limitation, it should be unique as well as not null. Let's create a few tables using primary key constraints:

```
warehouse_db=# CREATE TABLE tools
  (
```

```
tool_id INTEGER PRIMARY KEY,
tool_name TEXT,
tool_class NUMERIC
);
```

You can also create a primary key constraint based on two columns. Consider the following example:

```
warehouse_db=# CREATE TABLE tools
(
tool_id INTEGER,
tool_name TEXT,
tool_class NUMERIC,
PRIMARY KEY (tool_id, tool_name)
);
```

Foreign key constraints

Foreign key constraints state that the value in a column must be the same as the value present in another table's row. This is for the sake of maintaining the referential integrity between two interlinked tables. Consider the following examples to understand the concept of foreign key constraints. We will create two tables, and we will use the column of one table in the second table as a foreign key constraint:

```
warehouse_db=# CREATE TABLE tools
(
tool_id INTEGER PRIMARY KEY,
tool_name TEXT,
tool_class NUMERIC
);
```

This will create a table with primary key constraints:

```
warehouse_db=# CREATE TABLE tools_list
(
list_id INTEGER PRIMARY KEY,
tool_id INTEGER REFERENCES tools (tool_id),
list_name TEXT
);
```

In the preceding query, we created a table with the name of tools_list that has a foreign key on the tool_id column with the tool_id reference column from the tools table.

A table can have multiple parent tables, which means that we can have more than one foreign key in a single table.

Check constraints

A **check constraint** lets you define a condition that a column must fulfill a Boolean expression. Let's understand this with some examples:

```
warehouse_db=# CREATE TABLE tools
  (
  tool_id INTEGER PRIMARY KEY,
  tool_name TEXT,
  tool_class NUMERIC,
  tool_quantity NUMERIC CHECK (tool_quantity > 0)
  );
```

In the preceding query, we have created a table with check constraints on tool_quantity to make sure that it must be greater than 0.

You can also give your constraints a more user-friendly name, so see the following example in which we name the constraint positive_quantity:

```
warehouse_db=# CREATE TABLE tools
  (
  tool_id INTEGER PRIMARY KEY,
  tool_name TEXT,
  tool_class NUMERIC,
  tool_quantity NUMERIC
  CONSTRAINT positive_quantity CHECK
  (tool_quantity>0)
  );
```

Privileges in PostgreSQL

In PostgreSQL, multiple privileges are present for every object that is created. By default, the owner (or a superuser) of an object has all the privileges on it. In PostgreSQL, the following types of privileges are present:

- SELECT
- INSERT
- UPDATE

- DELETE
- TRUNCATE
- REFERENCES
- TRIGGER
- CREATE
- CONNECT
- TEMPORARY
- EXECUTE
- USAGE

There are different privileges associated with different objects. For instance, the EXECUTE privilege is associated with procedure. The GRANT command is used to grant any privilege to any user. Similarly, to take back privileges, the REVOKE command is used.

Summary

In this chapter, we learned how to utilize the SQL language for a collection of everyday **Database Management System (DBMS)** exercises in an easy-to-use practical way. We figured out how to make a complete warehouse_db database that incorporates DDL (create, alter, and truncate) and DML (insert, update, and delete) operators, all types of data types, and constraints. The knowledge learned in this chapter will allow you to easily manipulate data across different tables and help you successfully design a database.

In the next chapter, you will learn about the procedural languages in more detail.

2
The Procedural Language

In the previous chapter, you saw what wonders you can do with SQL, but there is still some more magic left to show you, so let's investigate SQL further.

Before we begin, let's first consider and compare what you would choose to do:

- Execute individual SQL statements again and again, which involves numerous server round trips, or even worse if it's over long-distance networks
- Execute blocks of code that are stored in the DBMS, which serve the same purpose without involving those server round trips

The second option seems to be an obvious choice. Luckily, this block of code is actually a procedural language. In the case of PostgreSQL, this procedural language is named **Procedural Language/PostgreSQL (PL/pgSQL)**.

PL/pgSQL is to PostgreSQL what PL/SQL is to Oracle (or what Transact/SQL is to Microsoft SQL Server). Procedural languages can be used to write functions, and in PL/pgSQL, function is a labeled sequence of statements written inside an SQL expression. By doing so, you are actually extending the server. These server extensions are also known as **stored procedures**. This is why we're going to learn about this now.

Based upon this, here is what you will learn in this chapter:

- What is a procedural language?
- PL/pgSQL language, conceptual elements, declarations, writing functions, control structures, and exception handling
- Interfacing through other procedural languages, namely PL/Python, PL/Tcl, and PL/Perl

Why should you use PL/pgSQL?

SQL statements are executed individually, so your query is sent one by one to the server to be parsed, processed, and returned as the result. Doing this occasionally is not an issue but when you have to execute thousands of queries each day, you can simply write a PL/pgSQL function. More specifically, this is a stored procedure that can perform all SQL instructions using any of the **loop** control structures available. Loop control structures such as WHILE and FOR, will be executed on the decision of various conditional structures used along with the variables that are declared to store the results and even process these results later. Additionally, it can handle **errors** and **exceptions** as well.

PL/pgSQL encapsulates an expression style of SQL and implements programming concepts such as other languages.

You can write these functions in a variety of available languages, which for example can be Perl, Python, Java, and so on. Functions written in PL/pgSQL can invoke other functions or contain sub-blocks inside the main block.

With this much extensibility, it does not need to be mentioned that performance will certainly be improved.

Installing PL/pgSQL

You should make sure that you have installed the procedural language you are about to use. PostgreSQL supports many procedural languages, and it ensured that the installation process became seamless.

> You can consult the PostgreSQL manual present online at http://www.postgresql.org/docs/9.4/static/index.html for general syntax of statements, declarations, functions, and so on. In fact, this will also serve as a source for an in-detail study of PostgreSQL features and usage.

Simply launch the command-line utility and execute the following command:

```
$ createlang plpgsql database-name
```

> PL/pgSQL is installed by default and executing the preceding command might result in telling you that the language is already installed.

Suppose we have to install PL/pgSQL inside the `warehouse_db` database. Then, you will execute the following command (the Linux shell is used in this example):

```
$ createlang plpgsql warehouse_db
```

The preceding command assumes that the operating system username is the same as that of database **superuser**. If this is not the case, give the database superuser name at the end using the `-U` switch as follows:

```
$ createlang plpgsql warehouse_db -U postgres
```

 You don't need to insert a semicolon at end, as it's not an SQL command but rather an invocation via the command-line utility to the `createlang` shell script that loads the procedural language in the database.

Understanding the structure of PL/pgSQL

PL/pgSQL is a block-structured and case-insensitive language. A block comprises statements inside the same set of the `DECLARE`/`BEGIN` and `END` statements.

A block can be defined as follows:

```
DECLARE
   declarations
BEGIN
   statements
END;
```

We will jump to writing functions from here on, where these blocks play an integral part. Let's start decomposing the structure of function and then understand each element one by one.

The `CREATE FUNCTION` command is used to create the functions by first naming the function and defining its argument and return type, followed by the `declarations` section. Its syntax is as follows:

```
CREATE OR REPLACE FUNCTION function_name (arguments)
RETURNS type AS
```

 Remember that `CREATE OR REPLACE FUNCTION` is the best practice to follow than the simple `CREATE FUNCTION` command. The first one drops the function with same name if it exists and then recreates your function.

Inside the declaration section of the block, variables are declared, sometimes with an optional default value. This section is identified by the DECLARE keyword. The declaration section contains a variable name and its data type ends with a semicolon. Any variable, row, or records used in a block or its sub-block should be declared here, with an exception to the FOR loop. This can be represented as follows:

```
DECLARE
    declaration;
```

You have defined the function name with its return type and declared variables as well, so let's now start looking at the main body of the function with the BEGIN keyword. Its syntax is as follows:

```
BEGIN
    Statement;
```

The Statement section can further contain unlimited sub-blocks. The nested code blocks are read and interpreted as normal blocks and should be written using same methods done for normal PL/pgSQL blocks. In other words, start with the DECLARE keyword, followed by the BEGIN keyword, then the body of statements, and finally end with the END keyword.

 Remember that BEGIN/END does not start or stop any transaction but used for grouping of statements.

The END keyword ends the code block as shown in the following statement:

```
END;
LANGUAGE 'plpgsql';
```

The main body of a PL/pgSQL function should return a value of the type defined earlier and end any sub-block before the flow reaches the END keyword.

Let's start writing a function in PL/pgSQL.

The getRecords() function in the following example will simply return the total number of records present in the warehouse_tbl table of the warehouse_db database. This is the same database we created in the previous chapter:

```
CREATE OR REPLACE FUNCTION getRecords()
RETURNS INTEGER AS $$
DECLARE
    total INTEGER;
BEGIN
    SELECT COUNT(*) INTO total FROM warehouse_tbl;
```

```
        RETURN total;
    END;
    $$ LANGUAGE plpgsql;
```

Assuming that the `warehouse_tbl` table contains a few rows, launch the `psql` utility, connect to the `warehouse_db` database, and start the execution of the preceding code from scratch in the following manner:

```
./psql -U postgres -d warehouse_db -p 5432
```

Here, the `postgres` keyword is the default user and `5432` is the default port for a PostgreSQL installation.

Now, we can create the `getRecords()` function using the following statement:

```
warehouse_db=# CREATE OR REPLACE FUNCTION getRecords()
RETURNS INTEGER AS $$
DECLARE
  total INTEGER;
BEGIN
  SELECT COUNT(*) INTO total FROM warehouse_tbl;
  RETURN total;
END;
$$ LANGUAGE plpgsql;
```

The function has been created; now call it to see the result using the following statement:

```
warehouse_db=# SELECT getRecords();
 getRecords
------------
          1
(1 row)
```

Using comments in PL/pgSQL

Comments can be used in the same way in PL/pgSQL as in other languages. You can either use single-line comments, such as starting with two dashes and with no end character, as shown in the following format:

```
- - single line comment style
```

Otherwise, use the multiline style, such as the following format:

```
/* comments here */ for multi line comments block i.e.
/*
```

```
multi line
comment
style
*/
```

The following is an example of a PL/pgSQL function that explains about the usage of comments. You can see how comments increase the readability and make it comprehensible for anyone going through the block. Comments will surely help you recall the purpose of the code if you revisit it after a long time.:

```
warehouse_db=# CREATE OR REPLACE FUNCTION concat (text, text)
--
--This function will concatenate the two strings.
--
/* pipe characters are used to
Concatenate
the strings */
RETURNS text AS $$
BEGIN
   RETURN $1 || ' ' || $2;
END;
$$ LANGUAGE plpgsql;
```

The following statement shows the result:

```
warehouse_db=# SELECT concat('ware', 'house');
   concat
------------
 ware house
(1 row)
```

Declaring variables in PL/pgSQL

We know variables are used to store data. PL/pgSQL allows you to use variables to achieve this. Each variable is thus used in the lifetime of a block and must be declared within the DECLARE block starting with the DECLARE keyword.

Let's take a few lines from the getRecords() function we used earlier, as follows:

```
CREATE OR REPLACE FUNCTION getRecords()
RETURNS integer AS $$
Declare
   total INTEGER;
```

We can see that the total variable is declared with its INTEGER data type before it stores the result returned to it.

 The following is the general syntax for declaring a variable:

```
name [ CONSTANT ] type [ COLLATE collation_name ] [ NOT
    NULL ] [ { DEFAULT | := } expression
```

Adding a variable with the CONSTANT keyword makes sure that the variable's values will remain constant during the execution of the block.

The COLLATE keyword defines the collation to be used for variable.

Variables can be declared with a default value; if they are not given a default value, they are assigned a null value. You can also use the := operator that carries the same meaning as using the DEFAULT keyword.

NOT NULL is the case where you do not want to set the value of a variable as null, and doing so in the block section can lead to a runtime error.

 As a good programming practice, a variable declared as NOT NULL should be given a default value.

It should be remembered that each time a block is executed, default values are evaluated and assigned so. This is further explained with the help of a PL/pgSQL function that contains variables using the DEFAULT, CONSTANT, and NOT NULL options.

The func_declare() function in the following example shows the declaration of a CONSTANT variable with its default value as 10. The declaration of a variable with NOT NULL is also initialized with a default value and the declaration of a character variable with the DEFAULT value:

```
warehouse_db=# CREATE OR REPLACE FUNCTION func_declare()
RETURNS text AS $$
DECLARE
-- Variable store declared not null with a default value.
nanvar VARCHAR NOT NULL := 'notnull text';
-- Declaring an integer to hold integer constant.
digit CONSTANT INTEGER := 10;
/* declaring variable with
a default value.*/
helloworld VARCHAR DEFAULT 'PostgreSQL rocks !';
BEGIN
```

```
    RETURN helloworld;
END;
$$ LANGUAGE 'plpgsql';
```

The result can be seen using the following statement:

```
warehouse_db=# SELECT func_declare();
    func_declare
-------------------
    PostgreSQL rocks !
(1 row)
```

Declaring function parameters

Functions can accept and return values called **function parameters** or **arguments**. These parameters should be declared before usage.

Parameters thus passed to functions are labeled with the numeric identifiers $1 and $2. We can also use an **alias** for a parameter name; both can then be later used to reference the parameter value.

You can explicitly declare an alias as well, as shown in the following statement:

```
name ALIAS FOR $n;
```

A more detailed explanation of the preceding statement is as follows:

```
CREATE OR REPLACE FUNCTION alias_explain(int)
RETURNS integer AS $$
DECLARE
    total ALIAS FOR $1;
BEGIN
    RETURN total*10;
END;
$$ LANGUAGE plpgsql;
```

The more common format is the one where you give a name to the parameter in the CREATE FUNCTION command, shown as follows:

```
CREATE OR REPLACE FUNCTION alias_explain(total int)
RETURNS integer AS $$
BEGIN
    RETURN total*10;
END;
$$ LANGUAGE plpgsql;
```

The result of the preceding formats can be seen using the following statement:

```
warehouse_db=# SELECT alias_explain(10);
 alias_explain
---------------
           100
(1 row)
```

We have seen how to alias a parameter; now let's see the types of parameters. They are IN, OUT, and INOUT. A function declared with the IN parameters contains a value that can be passed to a function.

 Remember that if not mentioned explicitly, function parameters are IN by default.

The OUT parameters are the ones that get returned as the result. They are effective when you have to return lots of output from a function without declaring the PostgreSQL type as output of the function.

 You can use the RETURNS statement in the CREATE FUNCTION statement with the OUT parameters but this would be redundant.

A function that is declared with the INOUT parameters serves both purposes — they can be passed in as well as processed and returned.

Let's look at the following function that explains the IN and OUT parameters:

```
warehouse_db=# CREATE OR REPLACE FUNCTION func_param(a int, IN b
                   int, OUT plus int, OUT sub int) AS $$
BEGIN
  plus := a + b;
  sub := a - b;
END;
$$ LANGUAGE plpgsql;
```

The result can be seen using the following statement:

```
warehouse_db=# SELECT func_param(10, 5);
 func_param
------------
 (15,5)
(1 row)
```

Declaring the %TYPE attribute

The `%TYPE` attribute is helpful to store values of a database object, usually a table column. This means declaring a variable with this attribute will store the value of the same data type it referenced. This is even more helpful if in future your column's data type gets changed. It's declared in the following manner:

```
variable_name table_name.column_name%TYPE
```

Using the `warehouse_db` database, we have a column name `amount` in the `history` table in the `record` schema. So, we can declare a variable referencing this column. This will look like the following:

```
amount history.history%TYPE
```

Declaring the row-type and record type variables

A row-type variable declares a row with the structure of an existing user-defined table or view using the `table_name%ROWTYPE` notation; otherwise, it can be declared by giving a composite type's name. The fields of the row can be accessed with the dot notation, for example, `rowvariable.field`.

The variable declared with `ROWTYPE` can store a row of a `SELECT` or `FOR` query result, as long as that query's column type matches with that of the variable declared. Record types are similar to row-types with the exception that they do not have any predefined structure and can accept a row from any table. This means that they can change their structure each time they are assigned to a row. They can be used in the `SELECT` and `FOR` commands to store database rows. Accessing it before it's assigned or if it contains any results will lead to a runtime error.

Statements and expressions

Statements and expressions are important constructs for any programming language. PL/pgSQL code is composed of a variety of statements and expressions. Remember that statements are commands that do not return a result and expressions evaluate to return a result. An expression can also be distinguished as an internal component of a statement and a very useful one for data manipulation.

Using statements

You use statements in the PL/pgSQL code whenever you are assigning a value to a variable, calling a function, or using conditions such as IF / ELSE.

The order of the execution of statements is controlled by the organization of statements. Within the space of the BEGIN and END blocks, the main chunk of statements are placed along with a few declarative statements in the DECLARE block as well.

[Remember that statements ends with a semicolon.]

The assignment statement

The assignment statement is the most common statement you will use in code. Assignment means assigning a value to a variable. Its syntax is as follows:

```
target := expression;
```

Here, target can be anything; it can be a variable, a column, a function parameter, or a row but not a constant. During execution, expression is first evaluated to a value when PL/pgSQL executes an assignment statement. It starts by evaluating expression and assigning the value to target. If the type for value and target mismatches, PostgreSQL converts the type accordingly or generates an error if the conversion is not possible.

You have already observed the examples of assignment statements; let's recall them:

- SELECT INTO usage in the getRecords() function:
  ```
  SELECT COUNT(*) INTO TOTAL FROM warehouse_tbl;
  ```

- Default value assignment in the func_param() function:
  ```
  plus := a + b;
  ```

The call/return function

All PostgreSQL functions return a value, and to call a function is to simply run a SELECT statement query or an assignment statement. The following are some of the examples:

- The SELECT statement in the function_identifier() function:
  ```
  SELECT function_identifier(arguments);
  ```

- Default value assignment in the `function_identifier()` function:

  ```
  variable_identifier := function_identifier(arguments);
  ```

- The `SELECT` statement in the `AVG(amount)` function:

  ```
  SELECT AVG(amount) FROM history;
  ```

- The `SELECT` statement in the `getRecords()` function:

  ```
  SELECT getRecords();
  ```

Similarly, values are returned with a `RETURN` statement.

The RETURN expression

As the function ends, the evaluated value of expression will be returned as per the specified return type in the `CREATE FUNCTION` command.

The syntax for the `RETURN` command is as follows:

```
CREATE OR REPLACE FUNCTION function_identifier(arguments)
RETURNS TYPE AS
DECLARE
  declaration;
BEGIN
  statement;
  RETURN { variable_name | value }
END;
LANGUAGE 'plpgsql';
```

Exception handling statements

Programming languages provide an exception handling mechanism to handle errors and reports for solution analysis. You can implement the `RAISE` statements to raise errors and exceptions in the PL/pgSQL function as follows:

```
RAISE NOTICE ''amount value is small.'';
```

 Error handling will be discussed later in this chapter.

Compound statements

Conditional or looping structures contain statements that are executed on the evaluation of conditions.

The syntax for conditional statements is as follows:

```
IF expression THEN
   Statements
ELSE
   Statements
END IF;
```

The syntax for looping statements is as follows:

```
LOOP
   Statements
END LOOP;
```

 Conditions and expressions will be explained in detail in the following sections.

Expressions

An expression can be a collection of one or more values, constants, variables, operators, and PostgreSQL functions that evaluate as per rules of a language, to a value that has a data type, which is one of the PostgreSQL base data types.

The following statement is an example of a Boolean expression; the part after the WHERE clause evaluates the matching expression:

```
SELECT * FROM history WHERE amount = 1000;
```

The following statement is an example of a numeric expression (one that involves mathematical calculation):

```
SELECT COUNT(*) FROM history;
```

Here, we used a built-in aggregate function that calculates all rows of the history table.

The examples of expressions for the INSERT and UPDATE statements are given as follows:

```
INSERT INTO table VALUES( expression [,...] );
INSERT INTO warehouse_tbl
  (
  warehouse_id,
  warehouse_name,
  year_created,
  street_address,
```

```
          city,
          state,
          zip
          )
VALUES
          (
          2,
          'Bill & Co',
          2014,
          'Lilly Road',
          'New London',
          'CT',
          4321
          );
       UPDATE table SET column = expression [, ...] [WHERE condition]
       UPDATE warehouse_tbl SET street_address = 'Tulip Road' WHERE
          street_address='Lilly Road';
```

Evaluation of expressions is actually done by the PostgreSQL server and not PL/pgSQL. All PL/pgSQL expressions are prepared only once during the lifetime of a PostgreSQL backend process.

Control structures

The strength of a programming language can also be judged by the means it provides to control the flow of a program. It's a structural organization of statements in such a way that it should determine the order of execution. Conditional statements and loops are one of those options. PL/pgSQL is fortunate to have these features as well, thus giving its users the freedom to code and control.

Conditional statements

Conditional statements execute in true sense of their literal meanings. It means that they perform a specified operation only when a certain defined condition is met. Hence, in this way, the logical resolution of the condition decides the flow of the program.

Let's dissect the conditional statements of PL/pgSQL one by one and see how much versatility each statement depicts.

IF-THEN

IF-THEN statements are the simplest of all IF-ELSE forms. The syntax of an IF-THEN statement is as follows:

```
IF boolean-expression THEN
   Statements
END IF;
```

The fate of statements between the THEN and END block depends on the successful evaluation of the boolean-expression to be true; otherwise, this block will be ignored.

The following example could be one of the scenarios to update the warehouse_tbl table for certain criteria to be true:

```
IF warehouse_id > 2 THEN
   UPDATE warehouse_tbl
   SET street_address='Tulip Road'
   WHERE street_address='Lilly Road';
END IF;
```

IF-THEN-ELSE

Now what if you have reached a point where you want your program to choose an alternate course of action if it fails to meet the criteria for one, rather than simply quitting. IF-THEN-ELSE statements takes care of this. The ELSE part will be executed when the IF part fails to execute and vice versa. Its syntax is as follows:

```
IF boolean-expression THEN
   Statements
ELSE
   Statements;
END IF;
```

Let's modify the getRecords() function we created earlier and add an IF-THEN-ELSE block as follows:

```
warehouse_db=# CREATE OR REPLACE FUNCTION getRecords()
RETURNS INTEGER AS $$
DECLARE
   total INTEGER;
BEGIN
   SELECT COUNT(*) INTO total FROM warehouse_tbl;
   IF (total > 0) THEN
     RETURN total;
   ELSE
```

```
        RAISE NOTICE 'table is empty';
    END IF;
END;
$$ LANGUAGE plpgsql;
```

The result can be seen using the following statement:

```
warehouse_db=# SELECT getRecords();
 getRecords
------------
          3
(1 row)
```

IF-THEN-ELSIF

If the case is of more than two alternatives to have in an IF-ELSE structure, then IF-THEN-ELSIF will be the solution. The IF condition is tested until a successful IF clause provides a true result, followed by the execution of associated statements and finally passing control to the statement after END IF. This can be explained with the help of the following example:

```
warehouse_db=# CREATE OR REPLACE FUNCTION nest_if(marks integer)
RETURNS text AS $$
DECLARE
   grade text;
BEGIN
   IF marks > 33 THEN
     grade := 'PASS';
     RETURN grade;
   ELSIF marks = 33 THEN
     grade := 'Average' ;
     RETURN grade;
   ELSIF marks < 33 THEN
     grade := 'FAIL';
     RETURN grade;
   ELSE
-- this means he did not appear in exam
     grade := 'DID NOT APPEAR IN EXAM';
     RETURN grade;
   END IF;
END;
$$ LANGUAGE plpgsql;
```

The result with 33 marks can be seen using the following statement:

```
warehouse_db=# SELECT nest_if(33);
 nest_if
---------
 Average
(1 row)
```

The result with 32 marks can be seen using the following statement:

```
warehouse_db=# SELECT nest_if(32);
 nest_if
---------
    FAIL
(1 row)
```

The result with 34 marks can be seen using the following statement:

```
warehouse_db=# SELECT nest_if(34);
 nest_if
---------
    PASS
(1 row)
```

Simple CASE

The CASE statement helps executing conditions on equality of operands. The search-expression is evaluated first and matched with each expression in the WHEN clause. When a match is found, associated statements will be executed and control will be transferred to the next statement after END CASE. If no match is found amongst the WHEN clauses, the ELSE block will be executed.

 If no match is found and ELSE is also absent, it will raise a CASE_NOT_FOUND exception.

Here is the syntax for a simple CASE statement:

```
CASE search-expression
  WHEN expression THEN
    Statements
END CASE;
```

Let's implement the nest_if() function for CASE:

```
warehouse_db=# CREATE OR REPLACE FUNCTION simple_case(marks
                 integer)
RETURNS text AS $$
DECLARE
  grade text;
BEGIN
  CASE marks
    WHEN 34,40 THEN
      grade := 'PASS';
      RETURN grade;
    WHEN 33 THEN
      grade := 'FAIL';
      RETURN grade;
    ELSE
      grade := 'Did not appear in exam';
      RETURN grade;
  END CASE;
END;
$$ LANGUAGE plpgsql;
```

The result with 33 marks can be seen using the following statement:

```
warehouse_db=# SELECT simple_case(33);
 simple_case
-------------
    FAIL
(1 row)
```

The result with 34 marks can be seen using the following statement:

```
warehouse_db=# SELECT simple_case(34);
 simple_case
-------------
    PASS
(1 row)
```

The result with 40 marks can be seen using the following statement:

```
warehouse_db=# SELECT simple_case(40);
 simple_case
-------------
    PASS
(1 row)
```

Searched CASE

The searched CASE statement executes a condition based on the result of the boolean-expression. This is quite similar to IF-THEN-ELSIF. The evaluation of the expression continues until it finds a match and then subsequent statements are executed. Control is then transferred to the next statement after END CASE.

The syntax for a searched CASE statement is as follows:

```
CASE
   WHEN boolean-expression THEN
      Statements
END CASE;
```

We will implement the same marks example in this as well in the following manner:

```
warehouse_db=# CREATE OR REPLACE FUNCTION search_case(marks
                  integer)
RETURNS text AS $$
DECLARE
   grade text;
BEGIN
   CASE
      WHEN marks >= 40 THEN
         grade := 'PASS';
         RETURN grade;
      WHEN marks <= 39 AND marks > 0 THEN
         grade := 'FAIL';
         RETURN grade;
      ELSE
         grade := 'Did not appear in exam';
         RETURN grade;
   END CASE;
END;
$$ LANGUAGE plpgsql;
```

The result with 30 marks can be seen using the following statement:

```
warehouse_db=# SELECT search_case(30);
 search_case
-------------
     FAIL
(1 row)
```

The result with 40 marks can be seen using the following statement:

```
warehouse_db=# SELECT search_case(40);
 search_case
-------------
     PASS
(1 row)
```

Loops

Match the condition, perform the desired task, and just keep doing this because you are executing loops. It is one of the powerful programming constructs that makes life easier when it comes to performing repetitive tasks on logical results of certain conditions. PL/pgSQL comes up with a variety of loop constructs that surely expands its scope to address and meet high-level requirements.

The simple loop

The simple loops are composed of an unconditional loop that ends only with an EXIT statement. Remember that EXIT can be used with all loop constructs, not only with an unconditional loop. The syntax for a simple loop is as follows:

```
LOOP
    Statements
END LOOP;
```

The syntax for EXIT is as follows:

```
EXIT WHEN boolean-expression;
```

If no label is given to an EXIT command, the innermost loop is terminated.

```
LOOP
   result = result-1;
   IF result > 0 THEN
     -- exits loop
     EXIT;
   END IF;
END LOOP;
```

The other way to use EXIT is as follows:

```
LOOP
   result = result -1
   EXIT WHEN result > 0;
END LOOP;
```

Let's implement this in the following PL/pgSQL function where `simple_loop()`, which takes a number of `subjects` as input, is multiplied with `grade`. The loop will iterate until the product of `grade` and `subjects` either equals `100` or becomes greater causing the loop to exit:

```
warehouse_db=# CREATE OR REPLACE FUNCTION simple_loop(subjects
                integer)
RETURNS integer AS $$
DECLARE
  grade integer := 10;
BEGIN
  LOOP
    grade := grade * subjects;
    IF (grade >= 100) THEN
      EXIT;
    END IF;
  END LOOP;
  RETURN grade;
END;
$$ LANGUAGE plpgsql;
```

Its result can be seen using the following statement:

```
warehouse_db=# SELECT simple_loop(10);
 simple_loop
-------------
         100
(1 row)
```

The WHILE loop

The `WHILE` loop will loop until the `boolean-expression` becomes false. The expression is evaluated first before executing the associated commands.

The syntax of the `WHILE` loop is as follows:

```
WHILE boolean-expression
LOOP
  Statements
END LOOP;
```

Let's implement the previous example with the `WHILE` loop as well:

```
warehouse_db=# CREATE OR REPLACE FUNCTION while_loop(subjects
                integer)
RETURNS integer AS $$
```

```
DECLARE
  grade integer := 10;
BEGIN
  WHILE grade <= 100
  LOOP
    grade := grade * subjects;
  END LOOP;
  RETURN grade;
END;
$$ LANGUAGE plpgsql;
```

The result can be seen using the following statement:

```
warehouse_db=# SELECT while_loop(5);
 while_loop
------------
        250
(1 row)
```

The FOR loop

Even if you are not familiar with the FOR loop, it is one of the most important loops and part of the PL/pgSQL implementation of the LOOP structures.

The syntax of the FOR loop is as follows:

```
FOR i in 1...10
LOOP
  Statements
END LOOP;
```

The FOR loop iterates over a range of integer values. An iterative integer is declared here and doesn't need to be declared in the DECLARE block. The life scope of this variable remains within the FOR loop and ends after the loop exits. By default, it iterates with a step of 1, unless specified in the BY clause. Iteration ranges in the upper and lower ranges are defined as two expressions. If the REVERSE clause is given, then the iterated value will not step up but will be subtracted. We will first implement a simple FOR loop using the same grade example, as follows:

```
warehouse_db=# CREATE OR REPLACE FUNCTION first_for_loop(subjects
                integer)
RETURNS integer AS $$
DECLARE
  grade integer := 2;
BEGIN
  FOR i IN 1..10
```

```
LOOP
   grade := grade * subjects;
END LOOP;
RETURN grade;
END;
$$ LANGUAGE plpgsql;
```

The result can be seen using the following statement:

```
warehouse_db=# SELECT first_for_loop(2);
 first_for_loop
----------------
          2048
(1 row)
```

You can also play with the REVERSE and BY clauses to create the FOR loop, as follows:

```
warehouse_db=# CREATE OR REPLACE FUNCTION second_for_loop(subjects
                integer)
RETURNS integer AS $$
DECLARE
   grade integer := 2;
BEGIN
   FOR i IN REVERSE 10..1 BY 2
   LOOP
      grade := grade * subjects;
   END LOOP;
   RETURN grade;
END;
$$ LANGUAGE plpgsql;
```

The result can be seen using the following statement:

```
warehouse_db=# SELECT second_for_loop(2);
 second_for_loop
----------------
          64
(1 row)
```

Now we will iterate over a dynamic query (that is unknown at the time of writing the function and processed on runtime) using the EXECUTE keyword in the following manner:

```
warehouse_db=# CREATE OR REPLACE FUNCTION for_loop_query(query
                VARCHAR)
RETURNS integer AS $$
DECLARE
```

```
  count integer := 0;
  table_records RECORD;
BEGIN
  FOR table_records IN EXECUTE query
  LOOP
    count := count + 1;
  END LOOP;
  RETURN count;
END;
$$ LANGUAGE 'plpgsql';
```

When we ran a query against this function on the `warehouse_tbl` table, it counts the rows brought by the `SELECT` query.

```
warehouse_db=# SELECT for_loop_query('SELECT * FROM
              record.warehouse_tbl');
 for_loop_query
----------------
              3
(1 row)
```

Exception handling

To err is coder!

People make mistakes everywhere, and programming is no exception to it. PL/pgSQL has so far shown that it contains strengths of a programming language, and it did not leave its users with a void when it comes to error handling.

Implementing `RAISE` statements takes care of error handling in an efficient manner with the options of `NOTICE`, `DEBUG`, and `EXCEPTION`. By defining the level of issues it should raise, it sends information to be displayed and logs it in PostgreSQL logs, which are usually in `/var/log/messages`.

The `RAISE` statement is a statement and allowed in the `statements` section of a PL/pgSQL block.

The syntax for a `RAISE` statement is as follows:

```
RAISE NOTICE|DEBUG|EXCEPTION ''your message string'';
```

The following is an example of a simple `RAISE` statement:

```
IF ( a is not an int ) then
  Return a;
Else
  Raise NOTICE 'a is integer, enter string';
```

You can use the % sign to display variables in your messages as well.

The following function will get all records from the `warehouse_tbl` table, and if it finds no rows, it will tell the user that the table is empty and also shows the variable's stored value, which will be 0 in the case when no rows exist.

For the sake of explanation, let's drop any rows present in the table using the following statement:

```
warehouse_db=# DELETE FROM warehouse_tbl;
```

Now, consider the following example using the `how_to_raise()` function in the `warehouse_tbl` table:

```
warehouse_db=# CREATE OR REPLACE FUNCTION how_to_raise()
RETURNS INTEGER AS $$
Declare
  total INTEGER;
BEGIN
  SELECT COUNT(*) INTO total FROM warehouse_tbl;
  IF (total > 0) THEN
    RETURN total;
  ELSE
    RAISE NOTICE 'table is empty, % , rows', total;
  END IF;
END;
$$ LANGUAGE plpgsql;
```

Execute the function in `psql` and observe the results:

```
warehouse_db=# SELECT how_to_raise();
NOTICE:  table is empty, 0, rows
ERROR:  control reached end of function without RETURN
CONTEXT:  PL/pgSQL function how_to_raise()
```

On the contrary, the EXCEPTION level will send the messages as ERROR to the client program and will also abort the statement that triggers the exception.

Suppose there are no rows present in the previous example; we will enter a row and raise an exception and then the statement will be aborted.

For the sake of explanation, let's drop any rows present in the table using the following statement:

```
warehouse_db=# DELETE FROM warehouse_tbl;
```

Now, the following example shows how the client program can abort a statement that triggers an exception:

```
warehouse_db=# CREATE OR REPLACE FUNCTION how_to_raise()
RETURNS INTEGER AS $$
DECLARE
  total INTEGER;
BEGIN
  SELECT COUNT(*) INTO total FROM warehouse_tbl ;
  IF (total > 0) THEN
    RETURN total;
  ELSIF (total = 0) THEN
    --inform user that table is empty
    RAISE NOTICE 'Table is empty. Currently, % , row', total;
    -- insert a row in table
    INSERT INTO warehouse_tbl
      (
      warehouse_id,
      warehouse_name,
      year_created,
      street_address,
      city,
      state,
      zip
      )
    VALUES
      (
      4,
      'Bill & Co',
      2014,
      'Lilly Road',
      'New London',
      'CT',
      4321
      );
    --raise exception level message and transaction will be
    aborted as well.
    RAISE EXCEPTION 'Transaction will be aborted';
  END IF;
END;
$$ LANGUAGE plpgsql;
```

The result can be seen using the following statement:

```
warehouse_db=# SELECT how_to_raise();
NOTICE:  Table is empty. Currently, 0, row
ERROR:  Transaction will be aborted
```

Native support for other procedural languages

PL/pgSQL is not the only procedural language available for PostgreSQL. It has native support for Python, Perl and Tcl as well. It doesn't stop here. However, it allows the usage of other procedural languages, for example, PL/Java and PL/Ruby. PostgreSQL uses **bison** (a parser generator) in the parsing process, thus enabling it to allow support for various open source languages.

In this section, we will skim through the usage of PostgreSQL native procedural languages such as PL/Python, PL/Perl, and PL/Tcl. We will learn how to write basic functions in these languages, pass arguments, and access a database.

Earlier, you saw that a language must first be installed to make it work. If you recall, the `createlang` shell script was used earlier to install PL/pgSQL. Now, you can also use the `CREATE EXTENSION database_name` query to install the other procedural languages.

> Do check the installation notes for your PostgreSQL installation to see which version of Python, Perl, and Tcl are compiled with the PostgreSQL version you are using. After installing the packages, make sure that they are added to system's PATH variable as well.

PL/Python

PL/Python is a procedural language that helps write stored functions in Python.

Installing PL/Python

The installation of PL/Python is fairly simple; launch the `psql` utility, connect to the `warehouse_db` database (created earlier), and execute the following command:

$ ./psql -U postgres -d warehouse_db

We can create an extension for Python using the following statement:

```
warehouse_db=# CREATE EXTENSION plpython3u;
```

Now that we have created an extension, let's start writing a simple Python function, and you will see that it won't be that different from the Python code style.

> If you face Python installation issues, don't worry you will surely land safely after some research.
>
> If you need some help, solutions for Python issues can be found at `http://raghavt.blogspot.com/2013/07/error-could-not-access-file.html`.

Writing functions in PL/Python

The `test_python()` function simply takes two arguments as integers, compares their values, and returns the respective result after evaluation. We will write more meaningful examples ahead.

> Be careful about indentation when programming in Python. You should learn by trying to disturb the indentation first and observe Python's behavior.

The following example makes use of the `test_python()` function:

```
warehouse_db=# CREATE OR REPLACE FUNCTION test_python(x integer,
                 y integer)
   RETURNS integer
AS $$
  if x < y:
    return x
  return y
$$ LANGUAGE plpython3u;
```

Execute the preceding command in the `psql` utility:

```
warehouse_db=# SELECT test_python(5,6);
 test_python
-------------
           5
(1 row)
```

Handling arguments with PL/Python

Now, let's write another simple function that takes `text` as input and returns `text` to the client program in the following manner:

```
warehouse_db=# CREATE OR REPLACE FUNCTION python_string(txtdata
                 text)
   RETURNS text
```

```
AS $$
  return 'PostgreSQL %s.' % txtdata
$$ LANGUAGE plpython3u;
```

The result can be seen using the following statement:

```
warehouse_db=# SELECT python_string('rocks');
  python_string
  ----------------
  PostgreSQL rocks
(1 row)
```

Accessing the database with PL/Python

We will now access the database through PL/Python using the `plpy.execute()` function that will take a `text` query as input and return a list of dictionaries as the result. The `warehouse_id` database will be sent as an argument to the `getRecords_withpython()` function that is further passed to `plpy.execute()`.This can be done in the following manner:

```
warehouse_db=# CREATE OR REPLACE FUNCTION
                getRecords_withpython(warehouse_id int)
  RETURNS text
AS $$
  res = plpy.execute("""
    SELECT * FROM warehouse_tbl
    WHERE warehouse_id = '%s'""" % warehouse_id)
  if res.nrows() > 0:
    return res
  else:
    return 'No rows found'
$$ LANGUAGE plpython3u;
```

Now, execute the code in `psql` using the following statement:

```
warehouse_db=# SELECT getRecords_withpython(1);
                getRecords_withpython
-------------------------------------------------------
<PLyResult status = 5 nrows = 1 rows = [{'city': 'New London',
  'zip': '4321', 'year_created': 2009, 'warehouse_id': 1, 'state':
  'CT', 'warehouse_name': 'Mark Corp', 'street_address': '207-F
  Main Service Road East'}]>
(1 row)
```

PL/Perl

The next language in the list of native languages of PostgreSQL is PL/Perl that also incorporates features to control the flow of the program.

Installing PL/Perl

Here, the CREATE EXTENSION method will be used by executing the following statement via the psql utility:

```
warehouse_db=# CREATE EXTENSION plperl;
```

Writing functions in PL/Perl

You can write a function in PL/Perl by following its simple syntax, as shown:

```
CREATE OR REPLACE FUNCTION name (arguments) RETURNS return-type AS
  $$
  # PL/Perl body(Perl code)
$$ LANGUAGE plperl;
```

 You can pass arguments to a PL/Perl function, and they can be accessed inside the function with the @_ array and can return results using return.

Let's write a function using the preceding syntax. The test_perl() function will simply return the txt value variable to a client program in the following manner:

```
warehouse_db=# CREATE FUNCTION test_perl() RETURNS text AS $$
  $txt='PostgreSQL Rocks !';
  return $txt;
$$ LANGUAGE plperl;
```

Handling arguments with PL/Perl

Now, we will pass arguments to a PL/Perl function and access them. The perl_arguments() function takes input from three arguments, executes a loop whose iteration depends upon the number of arguments (three times in this example), and calculates the sum of the a variable and the three integer arguments passed to the function:

```
warehouse_db=# CREATE OR REPLACE FUNCTION perl_arguments(INTEGER,
                INTEGER, INTEGER)
RETURNS INTEGER AS $$
  $a = 1;
  foreach $argument (@_){
```

```
    $a= $a + @_[0] + @_[1] + @_[2];
  }
  return $a;
$$ LANGUAGE plperl;
```

The result can be seen using the following statement:

```
warehouse_db=# SELECT perl_arguments(2,3,4);
 perl_arguments
----------------
             28
(1 row)
```

Accessing the database with PL/Perl

We will access the database using PL/Perl's `spi_exec_query` function. Suppose we want to retrieve one row from the `warehouse_tbl` table. Let's dig the code for this problem statement.

 PL/Perl functions can return the result set of scalar and composite types.

The `getRecords_withperl()` function returns `SETOF warehouse_tbl` using the `spi_exec_query()` function. The `rownumber` variable is used to reference the first row from corresponding rows in the result. The `return_next` query is used to return the rows one by one, though only one in the following case:

```
warehouse_db=# CREATE OR REPLACE FUNCTION getRecords_withperl()
RETURNS SETOF warehouse_tbl as $$
  $tblrow = spi_exec_query('SELECT warehouse_id, warehouse_name,
  state FROM warehouse_tbl ;');
  $rownumber = 0;
  $row = $tblrow->{rows}[$rownumber];
  return_next( $row );
$$ LANGUAGE plperl;
```

Let's execute the function in `psql` in the following manner:

```
warehouse_db=# SELECT warehouse_id, warehouse_name, state FROM
getRecords_withperl();
 warehouse_id | warehouse_name | state
--------------+----------------+------
            1 | Mark Corp      | CT
(1 row)
```

In our following example, we will implement a loop to iterate through a table and return the results one by one using `return_next`:

```
warehouse_db=# CREATE OR REPLACE FUNCTION
                getRecords_withperl_again()
RETURNS SETOF warehouse_tbl as $$
  my $tblrow = spi_exec_query('SELECT warehouse_id,
  warehouse_name, state FROM warehouse_tbl;');
  my $numberofrows = $tblrow->{processed};
  foreach my $rownumber (0 .. $numberofrows-1){
    my $row = $tblrow->{rows}[$rownumber];
  return_next($row);
  }
return undef;
$$ LANGUAGE plperl;
```

> For the last `return_next` statement, there should be either the `return` or `return undef` statement.

Assuming that the `warehouse_tbl` table has a few rows, we will execute this function on the `psql` command-line utility and observe its results in the following manner:

```
warehouse_db=# SELECT warehouse_id, warehouse_name, state FROM
getRecords_withperl_again();
 warehouse_id | warehouse_name | state
--------------+----------------+------
            1 | Mark Corp      | CT
(1 row)
```

PL/Tcl

Finally, PL/Tcl is last in our list of discussion for native procedural languages of PostgreSQL. We will explore how to install it, handle arguments, and access a database.

Installing PL/Tcl

Use the same `CREATE EXTENSION` method to create the PL/Tcl procedural language in the following manner:

```
warehouse_db=# CREATE EXTENSION pltcl;
```

Writing functions in PL/Tcl

The overall syntactical structure remains the same, except with the function body being the Tcl code. This is as follows:

```
CREATE OR REPLACE FUNCTION name (arguments)
RETURNS return-type AS $$
  # PL/Tcl code
$$ LANGUAGE plperl;
```

Why don't you try writing a function using the preceding syntax. The test_tcl() function will simply return the a variable that is initially assigned to a value using the Tcl syntax in the following manner:

```
warehouse_db=# CREATE OR REPLACE FUNCTION test_tcl()
RETURNS text AS $$
  set a "PostgreSQL Rocks."
  return $a;
$$ LANGUAGE pltcl;
```

The result can be seen using the following statement:

```
warehouse_db=# SELECT test_tcl();
     test_tcl
-----------------
 PostgreSQL Rocks.
(1 row)
```

Handling arguments with PL/Tcl

The tcl_arguments() function computes the sum of three variables passed as arguments. These variables are assigned to the arg variable as a list and iterated using foreach. One by one, each argument is added to get the total result. This can be done in the following manner:

```
warehouse_db=# CREATE OR REPLACE FUNCTION tcl_arguments(integer,
                  integer, integer)
RETURNS integer AS $$
  set arg [list $1 $2 $3]
  set plus 0
  foreach variable $arg {
    set plus [expr $plus + $variable]
  }
  return $plus
$$ LANGUAGE pltcl;
```

You can see that during the executing the preceding code, it calculates the sum of three variables correctly. The result can be seen using the following statement:

```
warehouse_db=# SELECT tcl_arguments(2,3,4);
 tcl_arguments
---------------
             9
(1 row)
```

Accessing the database with PL/Tcl

We will use the `spi_exec()` function whose return value is the number of rows a query affects.

Let's execute the function and observe results against the `warehouse_tbl` table.

The array option enables values to be stored in the associated array indexed by the column name. You can also use another variant of `spi_exec()` here, with no array option and loop variable, for example, `[spi_exec "SELECT * FROM warehouse_tbl"]`.

The following is an example using the `spi_exec()` function in the `warehouse_tbl` table:

```
warehouse_db=# CREATE OR REPLACE FUNCTION getRecords_withtcl()
RETURNS integer AS $$
  set res [spi_exec -array tblrows "SELECT * FROM
  warehouse_tbl"]
  return $res;
$$ LANGUAGE pltcl;
```

Now, try to execute the query on the `warehouse_tbl` table as follows:

```
warehouse_db=# SELECT getRecords_withtcl();
 getRecords_withtcl
--------------------
                  3
(1 row)
```

Summary

This chapter was aimed at helping you grasp the versatility of PostgreSQL for procedural languages in general and PL/pgSQL in particular. You can now write programs as well as simple SQL queries by learning PL/pgSQL's conceptual elements, declarations, writing functions, control structures, and error handling. You have also briefly explored interfacing with other native languages, namely PL/Python, PL/Perl, and PL/Tcl.

The next chapter will be about indexes, explaining its usage and importance in databases. Let's keep rolling!

3
Working with Indexes

An index is a structure utilized for quick data retrieval operations. In the database world, an index is associated with a table and used to efficiently locate data without having to investigate every row in a database table. If a table does not have an index, then a full table scan is needed to find a record, which is very costly in terms of disk I/O and CPU utilization. A full table scan is the process of sequentially reading every record from disk, checking against search criteria, and building a result set.

In this chapter, you will learn the following topics:

- What is an index?
- How to create an index
- What are the different types of indexes?
- How to use different index methods
- Index problems

What is an index?

An index amends the performance of database operations at the cost of extra replicas of data. As an index stores the extra copy of data for more speedy access, an index is the routine way to amend the performance of the database. In a nutshell, an index is a quick access path to a single row of a table in the database. A database index is similar to a book index where any specific information can be located by looking at the index page to avoid the full search of the book, which is an exhaustive operation. Similarly, a database index is created to minimize table traversal and maximize performance.

An index can be created utilizing a single column or multiple columns of a table. Once the index is created, then there is no further intervention needed; the index will be automatically updated on each DML operation on the table. After creating the index, it is the planner's decision to utilize the index in lieu of sequential scans based on cost.

When PostgreSQL executes a query, it must choose an execution strategy. The planner is the piece of software that is in charge of establishing the best strategy to perform an efficient search.

Suppose we have a table named item that contains columns of item_id, item_name, item_price, and item_data and contains millions of rows. Let's connect to the warehouse_db database via the psql command-line utility and create the item table in the following manner:

```
warehouse_db=# CREATE TABLE item
  (
  item_id INTEGER NOT NULL,
  item_name TEXT,
  item_price NUMERIC,
  item_data TEXT
  );
```

The result can be seen using the following statement:

```
warehouse_db=# SELECT item_name FROM item WHERE item_id = 100;
```

If we want to get the details of a specific item using the preceding query, then the whole table should be scanned to find the item whose item_id is 100, which is a serious performance issue. This problem can be solved using indexes.

The EXPLAIN QUERY command can be used to check which scan will be used for the query. This can be explained with the following example:

```
warehouse_db=# EXPLAIN SELECT * FROM table_name;
                    QUERY PLAN
----------------------------------------------------------
Seq Scan on table_name
    (cost=10000000000.00..10000000001.01 rows=1 width=76)
Planning time: 0.071 ms
```

How to create an index

The CREATE INDEX command is used to create an index; the basic syntax of creating an index on a table is as follows:

```
CREATE INDEX index_name ON table_name (column_name);
```

Here is an example of creating an index on the item_id column of the item table:

```
warehouse_db=# CREATE INDEX item_idx ON item (item_id);
```

The result can be seen using the following statement:

```
warehouse_db=# \di item_idx;
                List of relations
 Schema |   Name    | Type  |  Owner   | Table
--------+-----------+-------+----------+-------
 public | item_idx  | index | postgres | item
(1 row)
```

The index name is optional; if the index name is not specified, PostgreSQL generates the index name using the table name and the column name. In the preceding example, we have specified the index name. In the following example, PostgreSQL generates the index name using the table name and column name, which is item_item_id_idx:

```
warehouse_db=# CREATE INDEX ON item (item_id);
CREATE INDEX
```

The result can be seen using the following statement:

```
warehouse_db=# \di item_item_id_idx;
                List of relations
 Schema |       Name        | Type  |  Owner   | Table
--------+-------------------+-------+----------+-------
 public | item_item_id_idx  | index | postgres | item
(1 row)
```

Creating an index on a large table can take a long time; for example, in the preceding example, the query has to scan all the records and generate the index data. On a larger table, this process can take time.

An index requires additional disk space, so be careful when creating an index. Also, insert/delete/update incurs more processing to maintain the index data, and the type of index has a different impact on performance. For instance, B-tree indexes require tree rebalancing, which is quite heavy in terms of computational cost.

Here is the complete syntax for index creation:

```
CREATE [ UNIQUE ] INDEX [ CONCURRENTLY ]
    [ name ] ON table [ USING method ]
    ( { column | ( expression ) }
    [ COLLATE collation ] [ opclass ] [ ASC | DESC ]
    [ NULLS { FIRST | LAST } ] [, ...])
    [ WITH ( storage_parameter = value [, ... ] ) ]
    [ TABLESPACE tablespace ]
    [ WHERE predicate ]
```

Details on the complete syntax for index creation can be found at the official PostgreSQL documentation available online at the following link: http://www.postgresql.org/docs/9.4/static/sql-createindex.html.

How to drop an index

The DROP INDEX command is used to drop an existing index. Its basic syntax is as follows:

```
warehouse_db=# DROP INDEX index_name;
```

Dropping an index will not affect the rows of the table, but be careful since it will affect the performance of the database.

Types of indexes

A PostgreSQL database supports the single-column index, multicolumn index, partial index, unique index, expression index, implicit index, and concurrent index.

The single-column index

The single-column index is utilized when a table represents mostly a single category of data, or queries span around only a single category in the table. Normally, in a database design, tables represent a single category of data, so generally a single-column (category) index is utilized. Its syntax is as follows:

```
CREATE INDEX index_name ON table_name (column);
```

Take a look at the following example:

```
warehouse_db=# SELECT COUNT(*) FROM item WHERE item_id = 100;
 count
-------
   202
(1 row)
Time: 201.206 ms
```

In this example, the rows are required where item_id is 100. If there is no index defined, then the whole table will be scanned to find the rows where item_id is 100, which is an expensive operation. If you look closely, only a single column is utilized in the WHERE clause, thereby creating an index on a single column, which is item_id in the case of the preceding query. This optimizes that query.

Now, consider the following example:

```
warehouse_db=# CREATE INDEX item_index ON item (item_id);
```

The result can be seen using the following statement:

```
warehouse_db=# \d item;
              Table "item"
   Column    |        Type         | Modifiers
-------------+---------------------+-----------
 item_id     | integer             | not null
 item_name   | text                |
 item_price  | numeric             |
 item_data   | text                |
Indexes:
    "item_index" btree (item_id)
```

Now, we have created a B-tree index, item_index, on a table item's item_id column, so now we try the same SELECT query again and see how much time it takes after index creation.

Creating an index on a table reduces the SELECT query time drastically, as shown in the following output:

```
warehouse_db=# SELECT COUNT(*) FROM item WHERE item_id = 100;
 count
-------
   202
(1 row)
Time: 1.140 ms
```

There is an obvious timing difference with and without the index. The same query without the index took approximately 200 ms to execute, and the query after creating the index took approximately 1 ms.

> The \d table_name query is used to describe the table.
> The \timing query is used to display the query time.

The multicolumn index

In some cases, there are tables in a database that involve multiple categories of data. In such cases, a single-column index might not give good performance. In this situation, the multicolumn index is needed. PostgreSQL supports the multicolumn index. Its syntax is as follows:

```
CREATE INDEX index_name ON table_name (column1, column2);
```

The multicolumn index, which involves multiple columns in a query, helps optimize the queries; let's look at an example.

In this example, we will get the total number of records whose item_id is less than 200 and item_price is also 100; first, we try the query without an index on the table and note the query time in the following manner:

```
warehouse_db=# SELECT COUNT(*) FROM item WHERE item_id < 200 AND
                item_price = 100;
 count
-------
   202
(1 row)
Time: 1675.783 ms
```

Now, we will create a single-column index, try the same query in the following manner, and note down the query execution time:

```
warehouse_db=# CREATE INDEX item_single_index ON item (item_id);
```

The result can be seen using the following statement:

```
warehouse_db=# SELECT COUNT(*) FROM item WHERE item_id < 200 AND
                      item_price = 100;
 count
-------
   202
(1 row)
Time: 1604.328 ms
```

Finally, create a multicolumn index on the table, try the same query in the following manner, and note down the timing of the query:

```
warehouse_db=# CREATE INDEX item_multi_index ON item (item_id,
                      item_price);
```

The result can be seen using the following statement:

```
warehouse_db=# SELECT COUNT(*) FROM item WHERE item_id < 200 AND
                      item_price = 100;
 count
-------
   202
(1 row)
Time: 331.295 ms
```

The query times are as follows:

Without index	Single-column index	Multicolumn index
1675.783 ms	1604.328 ms	331.295 ms

We can observe the difference in the execution time of the preceding queries. The query without an index took 1675.783 ms, the query with a single-column index ran slightly faster and took 1604.328 ms, and the query with a multicolumn index ran much faster and took only 331.295 ms. Therefore, creating a single-column or multicolumn index depends on the nature of the queries used, so selecting a proper index can give a real performance boost.

 By default, an index is created in ascending order; to create an index in descending order, use DESC after the column name.

The partial index

The partial index is an index that applies only on the rows that complete the designated condition. Most of the time, the subset of the table is used in the queries. In this case, creating an index on the whole table is a waste of space and time consuming. We should consider creating an index on the subset of the table in this case. The rudimental reason to have a partial index is better performance by using the least amount of disk space as compared to creating an index on a whole table.

To create an index on the subset of the table, we use a partial index. The partial index can be created by specifying the WHERE condition during index creation as follows:

```
CREATE INDEX index_name ON table_name (column) WHERE (condition);
```

Suppose most of the queries use the subset of the item table where item_id is less than 106, and then creating an index on the whole item table is a waste of space. The optimal case is to create an index only on the first 100 rows of the warehouse_tbl table. In this case, the partial index can be created for the rows less than 100. This can be done in the following manner:

```
warehouse_db=# CREATE INDEX item_partial_index ON item (item_id)
               WHERE (item_id < 106);
```

The result can be seen using the following statement:

```
warehouse_db=# \d item;
             Table "item"
  Column    |        Type        | Modifiers
------------+--------------------+-----------
 item_id    | integer            | not null
 item_name  | text               |
 item_price | numeric            |
 item_data  | text               |
Indexes:
    "item_index" btree (item_id)
    "item_multi_index" btree (item_id, item_price)
    "item_partial_index" btree (item_id) WHERE item_id < 106
```

 A B-tree index supports up to 32 columns to join in a single index.

The unique index

A unique index can be created on any column; it not only creates an index, but also enforces uniqueness of the column. This is the most important index in a database design as it ensures data integrity and provides performance enhancements. There are multiple ways to create a unique index: using the CREATE UNIQUE INDEX command, by creating a unique constraint on the table, or by creating a primary key.

Here is an example of a unique index created by the CREATE UNIQUE INDEX command:

```
warehouse_db=# CREATE UNIQUE INDEX item_unique_idx ON item
                (item_id);
CREATE INDEX
Time: 485.644 ms
```

The result can be seen using the following statement:

```
warehouse_db=# \d item_unique_idx;
                List of relations
 Schema |       Name       | Type  |  Owner   | Table
--------+------------------+-------+----------+-------
 public | item_unique_idx  | index | postgres | item
(1 row)
```

We have discussed that we can create a unique index explicitly using the CREATE UNIQUE INDEX command and that it can be created implicitly by declaring a primary key on a table. Here is an example of an implicit creation of a unique index by creating a primary key on a table:

```
warehouse_db=# CREATE TABLE item
  (
  item_unique INTEGER PRIMARY KEY,
  item_name TEXT,
  item_price NUMERIC,
  item_data TEXT
  );
```

The result can be seen using the following statement:

```
warehouse_db=# \d item
                 Table "item"
   Column      |          Type           | Modifiers
---------------+-------------------------+-----------
 item_unique   | integer                 | not null
 item_name     | text                    |
 item_price    | numeric                 |
```

```
    item_data        | text                        |
Indexes:
    "item_pkey" PRIMARY KEY, btree (item_unique)
```

Here is an example of an implicit creation of a unique index by defining unique constraints:

```
warehouse_db=# ALTER TABLE item ADD CONSTRAINT primary_key UNIQUE
                (item_unique);
```

The preceding SQL statement alters the table and adds a unique constraint on the item table's item_id column, and this statement also implicitly creates a unique index (B-tree).

Here, we restart with the original table:

```
warehouse_db=# \d item;
                    Table "item"
   Column      |          Type           |  Modifiers
-------------+-------------------------+-----------
 item_unique | integer                 | not null
 item_name   | text                    |
 item_price  | numeric                 |
 item_data   | text                    |
Indexes:
    "item_pkey" PRIMARY KEY, btree (item_unique)
    "primary_key" UNIQUE CONSTRAINT, btree (item_unique)
```

The ALTER command adds a unique constraint to the item_id column and can be used as the primary key.

Explicitly creating an index using the CREATE INDEX command

We have discussed how a unique index can be implicitly created on a table, but there is a way to create a unique index explicitly using the already discussed CREATE INDEX command as follows:

```
warehouse_db=# CREATE TABLE item
  (
  item_id INTEGER PRIMARY KEY,
  item_name TEXT,
  item_price NUMERIC,
  item_data TEXT
  );
```

We create the unique index using the following statement:

```
warehouse_db=# CREATE UNIQUE INDEX idx_unique_id ON item
               (item_id);
CREATE INDEX
```

The result can be seen using the following statement:

```
warehouse_db=# \d item;
              Table "item"
   Column     |         Type          | Modifiers
--------------+-----------------------+----------
   item_id    | integer               | not null
   item_name  | text                  |
   item_price | numeric               |
   item_data  | text                  |
Indexes:
      "idx_unique_id" UNIQUE, btree (item_id)
```

In all cases, a unique index ensures the integrity of data and throws an error in the case of duplicity. This can be seen in the following example:

```
warehouse_db=# INSERT INTO item VALUES (1, 'boxing', 200,
                'gloves');
warehouse_db=# INSERT INTO item VALUES (1, 'hockey', 300,
                'shoes');
ERROR:  duplicate key value violates unique constraint "
        idx_unique_id "
DETAIL:  Key (item_id)=(104) already exists.
```

[Only B-tree, GiST, and GIN indexes support the unique index.]

The expression index

We have discussed the creation of an index on a table's column, but in some cases, there is a requirement to add an expression on one or more columns of the table. For example, if we want to search for a case-insensitive item name, then the normal way of doing this is as follows:

```
warehouse_db=# SELECT * FROM item WHERE UPPER(item_name) LIKE
                'COFFEE';
```

The preceding query will scan each row or table and convert `item_name` to uppercase and compare it with `COFFEE`; this is really expensive. The following is the command to create an expression index on the `item_name` column:

```
warehouse_db=# CREATE INDEX item_expression_index ON item
              (UPPER(item_name));
```

The result can be seen using the following statement:

```
warehouse_db=# \d item;
                 Table "item"
   Column    |        Type        | Modifiers
-------------+--------------------+----------
 item_id     | integer            | not null
 item_name   | text               |
 item_price  | numeric            |
 item_data   | text               |
Indexes:
    "item_expression_index" btree (upper(item_name::text))
```

An expression index is only used when the exact expression is used in a query as in the definition. In this example, we query the `item` table and did not use the expression, so the planner does not use the expression index. This can be seen as follows:

```
warehouse_db=# EXPLAIN SELECT item_name FROM item WHERE item_name
              = 'item-10';
                        QUERY PLAN
----------------------------------------------------------
 Seq Scan on item (cost=0.00..22759.00 rows=1 width=11)
    Filter: (item_name = 'item-10'::text)
(2 rows)
```

However, in this example, we used the same expression as in the index definition, so the planner selects that index in the following manner:

```
warehouse_db=# EXPLAIN SELECT item_name FROM item WHERE
              UPPER(item_name) = 'ITEM-10';
                        QUERY PLAN
----------------------------------------------------------
 Bitmap Heap Scan on item  (cost=107.18..8714.04 rows=5000
   width=11)
    Recheck Cond: (upper(item_name) = 'ITEM-10'::text)
        -> Bitmap Index Scan on item_expression_index
          (cost=0.00..105.93 rows=5000 width=0)
            Index Cond: (upper(item_name) = 'ITEM-10'::text)
(4 rows)
```

The implicit index

An index that is created automatically by the database is called an implicit index. The primary key or unique constraint implicitly creates an index on that column. The implicit index has already been discussed in the *The unique index* section earlier in this chapter.

The concurrent index

Building an index locks the table from writing or inserting anything in the table. During the creation process, a process table can be read without an issue, but write operations block till the end of the index building process. We have already discussed that index creation on a table is a very expensive operation, and on a sizeably huge table, it can take hours to build an index. This can cause difficulty in regards to performing any write operations. To solve this issue, PostgreSQL has the concurrent index, which is useful when you need to add indexes in a live database.

The syntax of a concurrent index is as follows:

```
CREATE INDEX CONCURRENTLY index_name ON table_name using
    btree(column);
```

The concurrent index is slower than the normal index because it completes index building in two parts. This can be explained with the help of the following example:

Time taken in creating a normal index `idx_id` using `CREATE INDEX`:

```
warehouse_db=# CREATE INDEX idx_id ON item (item_id);
```

Time: 8265.473 ms

Time taken in creating a concurrent index `idx_id` using `CREATE INDEX CONCURRENTLY`:

```
warehouse_db=# CREATE INDEX CONCURRENTLY idx_id ON
    item (item_id);
```

Time: 51887.942 ms

Index types

PostgreSQL supports the B-tree, hash, GiST, and GIN index methods. The index method or type can be selected via the `USING` method. Different types of indexes have different purposes, for example, the B-tree index is effectively used when a query involves the range and equality operators and the hash index is effectively used when the equality operator is used in a query.

Here is a simple example of how to use the index types:

```
warehouse_db=# CREATE INDEX index_name ON table_name USING
               btree(column);
```

The B-tree index

The B-tree index is effectively used when a query involves the equality operator (=) and range operators (<, <=, >, >=, BETWEEN, and IN).

The hash index

Hash indexes are utilized when a query involves simple equivalent operators only. Here, we create a hash index on the item table. You can see in the following example that the planner chooses the hash index in the case of an equivalent operator and does not utilize the hash index in the case of the range operator:

```
warehouse_db=# CREATE INDEX item_hash_index ON item USING
               HASH(item_id);
```

As discussed, the hash index is the best for queries that have equivalent operators in the WHERE clause. This can be explained with the help of the following example:

```
warehouse_db=# EXPLAIN SELECT COUNT(*) FROM item WHERE item_id =
               100;
                            QUERY PLAN
-----------------------------------------------------------------
 Aggregate  (cost=8.02..8.03 rows=1 width=0)
    -> Index Scan using item_hash_index on item  (cost=0.00..8.02
    rows=1 width=0)
         Index Cond: (item_id = 100)
(3 rows)
```

The hash index method is not suitable for range operators, so the planner will not select a hash index for range queries:

```
warehouse_db=# EXPLAIN SELECT COUNT(*) FROM item WHERE item_id >
               100;
                            QUERY PLAN
-----------------------------------------------------------------
 Aggregate  (cost=25258.75..25258.76 rows=1 width=0)
    -> Seq Scan on item  (cost=0.00..22759.00 rows=999900 width=0)
         Filter: (item_id > 100)
(3 rows)
```

To get the size of a table and an index, we can use the following:

```
SELECT pg_relation_size('table_name')
AS table_size,pg_relation_size('index_name') index_
size
FROM pg_tables WHERE table_name like 'table_name';
```

The GiST index

The Generalized Search Tree (GiST) index provides the possibility to create custom data types with indexed access methods. It additionally provides an extensive set of queries.

It can be utilized for operations beyond equivalent and range comparisons. The GiST index is lossy, which means that it can create incorrect matches.

The syntax of the GiST index is as follows:

```
warehouse_db=# CREATE INDEX index_name ON table_name USING
               gist(column_name);
```

Modules and extensions developed using GiST are `rtree_gist`, `btree_gist`, `intarray`, `tsearch`, `ltree`, and `cube`. Its complete details can be found at the following link:

`http://www.postgresql.org/docs/9.4/static/gist-examples.html`.

The GIN index

The GIN index can be introduced with the help of the following quote found at the following link:

`http://www.postgresql.org/docs/9.4/static/gin-intro.html`

"GIN stands for Generalized Inverted Index. GIN is designed for handling cases where the items to be indexed are composite values, and the queries to be handled by the index need to search for element values that appear within the composite items. For example, the items could be documents, and the queries could be searches for documents containing specific words"

Here is the syntax for the creation of a GIN index:

```
warehouse_db=# CREATE INDEX index_name ON table_name USING
               gin(column_name);
```

The GIN index requires three times more space than GiST, but is three times faster than GiST.

Let's take an example where we want to search a word from millions of words using partial matches. The GIN index is best suited for these kinds of queries:

```
warehouse_db=# CREATE EXTENSION pg_trgm;
```

After creating the `pg_trgm` extension, we create the `words` table using the following statement:

```
warehouse_db=# CREATE TABLE words(lineno INT, simple_words TEXT,
                special_words TEXT);
```

We can insert data into the `words` table using the following statement:

```
warehouse_db=# INSERT INTO words VALUES
                (generate_series(1,2000000), md5(random()::TEXT),
                md5(random()::TEXT));
```

Let's try to execute a query to search for the words that have `a31` in `simple_words` and `special_words` and note the execution time of the query as follows:

```
warehouse_db=# SELECT count(*) FROM words WHERE simple_words LIKE
                '%a31%' AND special_words LIKE '%a31%';
 count
-------
   116
(1 row)
Time: 1081.796 ms
```

Create a multicolumn index and try to execute the same query and note down the timing of the query in the following manner:

```
warehouse_db=# CREATE INDEX words_idx ON words (simple_words,
                special_words);
Time: 32822.055 ms
```

The result can be seen using the following statement:

```
warehouse_db=# SELECT count(*) FROM words WHERE simple_words LIKE
                '%a31%' AND special_words LIKE '%a31%';
 count
-------
   116
(1 row)
Time: 1075.467 ms
```

Now, create a GIN index on the table, execute the same query again, and note down the timings in the following manner:

```
warehouse_db=# CREATE INDEX words_idx ON words USING gin
               (simple_words gin_trgm_ops, special_words
               gin_trgm_ops);
CREATE INDEX
Time: 142836.712 ms
```

The result can be seen using the following statement:

```
warehousd_db=# SELECT count(*) FROM words WHERE simple_words LIKE
               '%a31%' AND special_words LIKE '%a31%';
 count
-------
   116
(1 row)
Time: 7.105 ms
```

Now from the following table, we can clearly see the performance improvement using the GIN index:

Time without an index	Time with multicolumn index	Time with the GIN Index
1081.796 ms	1075.467 ms	7.105 ms

More details on the GIN index can be found at `http://www.sai.msu.su/~megera/wiki/Gin`.

More details on `pg_trgm` and `gin_trgm_ops` can be found at `http://www.postgresql.org/docs/9.4/static/pgtrgm.html`.

Index bloating

As the architecture of PostgreSQL is based on MVCC, tables have the difficulty of dead rows. Rows that are not visible to any transaction are considered **dead rows**. In a continuous table, some rows are deleted or updated. These operations cause dead space in a table. Dead space can potentially be reused when new data is inserted. Due to a lot of dead rows, bloating occurs. There are various reasons for index bloating, and it needs to be fixed to achieve more performance, because it hurts the performance of the database. AUTO VACUUM is the best obviation from bloating, but it is a configurable parameter and can be incapacitated or erroneously configured. There are multiple ways to fix index bloating; hence, we will discuss the ways to avert this and their efficacy in the following sections.

To know more about MVCC, check out http://www.postgresql.org/docs/ current/static/mvcc-intro.html.

Dump and restore

In the case of bloating, the simplest way of prevention is to back up the table utilizing pg_dump, drop the table, and reload the data into the initial table. This is an expensive operation and sometimes seems too restrictive.

VACUUM

Vacuuming the table using the VACUUM command is another solution that can be used to fix the bloat. The VACUUM command reshuffles the rows to ensure that the page is as full as possible, but database file shrinking only happens when there are 100 percent empty pages at the end of the file. This is the only case where VACUUM is useful to reduce the bloat. Its syntax is as follows:

```
VACUUM table_name
```

The following example shows the usage of VACUUM on the item table:

```
warehouse_db=# VACUUM item;
```

The other way of using VACUUM is as follows:

```
warehouse_db=# VACUUM FULL item;
```

CLUSTER

As we discussed previously, rewriting and reordering of rows can fix the issue that can be indirectly achieved using dump/restore, but this is an expensive operation. The other way to do this is the CLUSTER command, which is used to physically reorder rows based on the index. The CLUSTER command is used to create a whole initial copy of the table and the old copy of the data is dropped. The CLUSTER command requires enough space, virtually twice the disk space, to hold the initial organized copy of the data. Its syntax is as follows:

```
CLUSTER table_name USING index_name
```

Some queries used to get the size/rows of the index and table are as follows:

```
warehouse_db=# CREATE TABLE table_name AS SELECT * FROM
               generate_series(1, 9999999) AS
               COLUMN_KEY;
SELECT 9999999
warehouse_db=# CREATE INDEX index_name ON table_name
               (column_key);
CREATE INDEX
warehouse_db=# SELECT table_len/(1024*1024) table_size,
               tuple_count total_rows FROM
               pgstattuple('table_name');
 table_size | total_rows
------------+------------
        345 |    9999999
(1 row)
warehouse_db=# SELECT table_len/(1024*1024) table_size,
               tuple_count total_rows FROM
               pgstattuple('index_name');
 table_size | total_rows
------------+------------
        214 |    9999999
(1 row)
```

Reindexing

If an index becomes inefficient due to bloating or data becomes randomly scattered, then reindexing is required to get the maximum performance from the index. Its syntax is as follows:

```
warehouse_db=# REINDEX TABLE item;
```

Points to ponder

When using an index, you need to keep in mind the following things:

- It will make sense to index a table column when you have a handsome number of rows in a table.

- When retrieving data, you need to make sure that good candidates for an index are foreign keys and keys where min() and max () can be used when retrieving data. This means column selectivity is very important to index effectively.

- Don't forget to remove unused indexes for better performance. Also, perform REINDEX on all indexes once a month to clean up the dead tuples.

- Use table partitioning along with an index if you have large amounts of data.

- When you are indexing columns with null values, consider using a conditional index with WHERE column_name IS NOT NULL.

Summary

The major goal of this chapter was to explain the significance of index and index creation. An index represents the portion of a table, so it amends the read performance. You learned that PostgreSQL supports multiple types of single/ multicolumn index, partial index, expression index, and concurrent index. We also learned that PostgreSQL supports the B-tree, hash, GiST, and GIN index methods. An index adds overhead on every insert and update operation, and on every SELECT query, an index speeds up the searches. We saw that index building is a very expensive operation, and on a very huge table, it can take hours to complete, so the concurrent index can avail in that case, and we need to be correct about our index to avoid any index bloating.

Next on the list are triggers, rules, and views. The next chapter will highlight their utilization, structure, and most importantly, how they differ as compared to aggregate functions.

Triggers, Rules, and Views

You have learned to code and use functions in *Chapter 2, The Procedural Language*. These functions were called explicitly using the SELECT function() command. When a database grows, so does the complexity. You can't be there all time to monitor, implement, or troubleshoot what your database should do before or after a specific database event. For example, you do not want your customers to enter values against specific constraints you defined, or on inserting, updating, and deleting values, you want to have a function that can take care of modifications that have been made and make audit logs of all such operations.

A function with the capability to execute on its own when a certain event occurs is called a **trigger function**; this is executed when a trigger is fired against a specific database event.

In PostgreSQL, we have **rules**; certain tasks that can be done with triggers are achieved by these rules. Rules are used to implement views in PostgreSQL. **Views** are virtual tables that help to group data from one or more tables.

This chapter is important as it helps us to learn and understand how triggers, rules, and views can be significant in a database design. Understanding their meaning and significance is the key to their appropriate usage.

This chapter will cover the following topics:

- Triggers — creating trigger functions and usage
- Creating trigger functions in native PostgreSQL languages
- What PostgreSQL rules are and triggers versus rules
- Views — creating views and materialized views

Understanding triggers

A trigger, in terms of databases, means a certain operation to be performed spontaneously for a specific database event. For example, this event can be INSERT, UPDATE, or DELETE. So, by defining a trigger, you are defining certain operation(s) to be performed whenever that event occurs. An operation that a trigger refers to is called a trigger function.

Defining a trigger and defining a trigger function are two different things. The first can be created using CREATE TRIGGER and the latter can be created using the CREATE FUNCTION command. If the first one says what task to perform, the latter says how to perform this task.

You have to define a trigger function first before creating a trigger.

The following example is an abstract-level code to show how a trigger function and a trigger are written. You can write a trigger function in PL/pgSQL or any PostgreSQL-compatible language, for example, PL/Python and PL/Perl. This example uses PL/pgSQL:

```
CREATE OR REPLACE FUNCTION trigger_function_name
RETURNS trigger AS $SAMPLE_CODE$
BEGIN
/* your code goes here*/
  RETURN NEW;
END;
$SAMPLE_CODE$ LANGUAGE plpgsql;
```

 You can refer to the online PostgreSQL manual at http://www. postgresql.org/docs/9.4/static/index.html for a detailed reference on general syntax and in-depth explanation of the implementation of trigger, rules, and views.

The simple form of the CREATE TRIGGER syntax is as follows:

```
CREATE TRIGGER trigger_name {BEFORE | AFTER | INSTEAD OF} {event
  [OR ...]}
  ON table_name
  [FOR [EACH] {ROW | STATEMENT}]
  EXECUTE PROCEDURE trigger_function_name
```

So, a trigger function is a function but with the difference that it does not take arguments such as ordinary functions but through a special data structure called **TriggerData**; its return type is trigger, and it is automatically invoked when an event occurs that can be INSERT, UPDATE, DELETE, or TRUNCATE.

PostgreSQL comes with two main types of triggers: **row-level trigger** and **statement-level trigger**. These are specified with FOR EACH ROW (row-level triggers) and FOR EACH STATEMENT (statement-level triggers). The two can be differentiated by how many times the trigger is invoked and at what time. This means that if an UPDATE statement is executed that affects 10 rows, the row-level trigger will be invoked 10 times, whereas the statement-level trigger defined for a similar operation will be invoked only once per SQL statement.

Triggers can be attached to both tables and views. Triggers can be fired for tables before or after any INSERT, UPDATE, or DELETE operation; they can be fired once per affected row, or once per SQL statement. Triggers can be executed for the TRUNCATE statements as well. When a trigger event occurs, the trigger function is invoked to make the appropriate changes as per the logic you have defined in the trigger function.

The triggers defined with INSTEAD OF are used for INSERT, UPDATE, or DELETE on the views. In the case of views, triggers fired before or after INSERT, UPDATE, or DELETE can only be defined at the statement level, whereas triggers that fire INSTEAD OF on INSERT, UPDATE, or DELETE will only be defined at the row level.

Triggers are quite helpful where your database is being accessed by multiple applications, and you want to maintain complex data integrity (this will be difficult with available means) and monitor or log changes whenever a table data is being modified.

The next topic is a concise explanation of tricky trigger concepts and behaviors that we discussed previously. They can be helpful in a database design that involves triggers.

Tricky triggers

In FOR EACH ROW triggers, function variables contain table rows as either a NEW or OLD record variable, for example, in the case of INSERT, the table rows will be NEW, for DELETE, it is OLD, and for UPDATE, it will be both. The NEW variable contains the row after UPDATE and OLD variable holds the row state before UPDATE.

Hence, you can manipulate this data in contrast to FOR EACH STATEMENT triggers. This explains one thing clearly, that if you have to manipulate data, use FOR EACH ROW triggers.

The next question that strikes the mind is how to choose between row-level AFTER and BEFORE triggers.

Well, if you want to modify new values of INSERT/UPDATE before being stored to the table, you should use the BEFORE trigger. If your logic requires that for a certain operation on the current table, it should modify other tables as well, it's time to choose AFTER triggers. The row-level AFTER triggers are certain about the final state whereas the row-level BEFORE trigger cannot view the final state. One explanation for this can be that you might end up changing the other tables but the original table does not allow you to reach the final desired state.

If the row-level BEFORE triggers and if you return a non-null value, it should match the structure of the table to be modified but if you return null, it will skip rest of the operations and any INSERT/UPDATE/DELETE operation will not be effective.

The return value of a statement-level BEFORE trigger and an AFTER trigger is ignored by PostgreSQL. So, you can return null from a row-level AFTER trigger.

If we have to categorize it with respect to tables and views, the following facts should be kept in mind:

- The statement-level BEFORE and AFTER triggers can be defined on tables and views
- The row-level BEFORE and AFTER triggers should only be defined on tables
- The row-level INSTEAD OF triggers should only be defined on views

Creating triggers and trigger functions with PL/pgSQL

It is time to see triggers in action. For the sake of understanding, we will write trigger functions in PL/pgSQL first and then advance our skills by writing in other native languages as well.

Let's stick to the warehouse_db database and the warehouse_tbl table that reside inside the record schema.

 The table you want to modify should exist in the same database as the table or view to which the trigger is attached.

We will define our problem first. Let's begin with an easy-to-understand example where we simply track records of any new row being inserted into the `warehouse_tbl` table. This example uses only one trigger, one trigger function, and another table to log changes inserted by a trigger. We can set the search path using the following statement:

```
warehouse_db=# set search_path='record';
```

Let's create the `warehouse_tbl` table now in the following manner:

```
warehouse_db=# CREATE TABLE warehouse_tbl
  (
  warehouse_id INTEGER NOT NULL,
  warehouse_name TEXT NOT NULL,
  year_created INTEGER,
  street_address TEXT,
  city CHARACTER VARYING(100),
  state CHARACTER VARYING(2),
  zip CHARACTER VARYING(10),
  CONSTRAINT "PRIM_KEY" PRIMARY KEY (warehouse_id)
  );
```

Now, create the `warehouse_audit` table in the following manner:

```
warehouse_db=# CREATE TABLE warehouse_audit
  (
  wlog_id INT NOT NULL,
  insertion_time TEXT NOT NULL
  );
```

Assuming that the `warehouse_tbl` table is empty, we will insert a few rows before we define any trigger and trigger function, as follows:

```
warehouse_db=# INSERT INTO warehouse_tbl
  (warehouse_id, warehouse_name, year_created, street_address,
  city, state, zip)
VALUES
  (1, 'Mark Corp', 2009, '207-F Main Service Road East', 'New
  London', 'CT', 4321);

warehouse_db=# INSERT INTO warehouse_tbl
  (warehouse_id, warehouse_name, year_created, street_address,
  city, state, zip)
VALUES
  (2, 'Bill & Co', 2014, 'Lilly Road', 'New London', 'CT', 4321);
```

To verify that the rows are inserted, use the following command:

```
warehouse_db=# SELECT warehouse_id, warehouse_name, state FROM
               warehouse_tbl;
 warehouse_id | warehouse_name | state
--------------+----------------+-------
            1 | Mark Corp      | CT
            2 | Bill & Co      | CT
(2 rows)
```

 You can find detailed references in the PostgreSQL manual, which is available at http://www.postgresql.org/docs/9.4/static/server-programming.html, about the PostgreSQL implementation of triggers in native procedural languages with syntax and code.

We have already discussed that the trigger function gets input through a specially passed TriggerData structure, which contains a set of local variables that we will use in our trigger functions. This set of variables includes OLD, NEW, and other variables that have TG_ at the start of their names, such as TG_WHEN, TG_TABLE_NAME.

Let's discuss these set of variables:

- NEW: This variable is of the RECORD type and contains the new row to be stored for the INSERT/UPDATE command in row-level triggers

- OLD: This variable is also of the RECORD type and stores the old row for the DELETE/UPDATE operation in row-level triggers

- TG_OP: This will contain one of the strings that informs you for which operation the trigger is invoked; the value can be INSERT, UPDATE, DELETE, or TRUNCATE

- TG_TABLE_NAME: This holds the name of the table for which the trigger is fired

- TG_WHEN: This will contain the string with the value of BEFORE, AFTER, or INSTEAD OF, as per the trigger's definition

After creating tables, define a trigger function called warehouse_audit_func that will log changes in the warehouse_audit table after an INSERT operation on the warehouse_tbl table:

```
warehouse_db=# CREATE OR REPLACE FUNCTION warehouse_audit_func()
RETURNS trigger AS $first_trigger$
BEGIN
  INSERT INTO warehouse_audit
    (wlog_id, insertion_time)
  VALUES
```

```
        (new.warehouse_id, current_timestamp);
    RETURN NEW;
END;
$first_trigger$ LANGUAGE plpgsql;
```

Now, we will define the trigger and bind it to the associated table `warehouse_tbl` as follows:

```
warehouse_db=# CREATE TRIGGER audit_trigger
    AFTER INSERT ON warehouse_tbl
    FOR EACH ROW
    EXECUTE PROCEDURE warehouse_audit_func();
```

Let's insert a row in the `warehouse_tbl` table and verify the changes in the `warehouse_audit` table:

```
warehouse_db=# INSERT INTO warehouse_tbl
    (warehouse_id, warehouse_name, year_created, street_address,
    city, state, zip)
VALUES
    (3, 'West point', 2013, 'Down Town', 'New London', 'CT', 4321);
```

We can see that the changes are logged in the `warehouse_audit` table after `INSERT` on the `warehouse_tbl` table. We will use a `SELECT` command to check whether the record was inserted in the `warehouse_audit` table.

The result can be seen using the following statement:

```
warehouse_db=# SELECT * FROM warehouse_audit;
 wlog_id |           insertion_time
---------+------------------------------
       3 | 2014-09-01 03:09:38.791989+05
(1 row)
```

Now to check whether the record is inserted in the `warehouse_tbl` table, use the following statement:

```
warehouse_db=# SELECT warehouse_id, warehouse_name, state FROM
                warehouse_tbl;
 warehouse_id | warehouse_name | state
--------------+----------------+-------
            1 | Mark Corp      | CT
            2 | Bill & Co      | CT
            3 | West point     | CT
(3 rows)
```

The preceding example is a good and easy one to start writing triggers but from a database design perspective, you should be aware that the user can perform UPDATE or DELETE operation as well. Therefore, the next example will teach you how to handle the INSERT, UPDATE, and DELETE operations in one trigger function.

Let's modify the warehouse_audit table and add another column named operation_detail. This column will store values for the respective operation INSERT, UPDATE, or DELETE.

Let's empty the warehouse_audit table first using the following statement:

```
warehouse_db=# DROP TABLE warehouse_audit CASCADE;
```

Create the warehouse_audit table again in the following manner:

```
warehouse_db=# CREATE TABLE warehouse_audit
  (
  wlog_id INT NOT NULL,
  insertion_time TEXT NOT NULL,
  operation_detail CHARACTER VARYING
  );
```

Now create a trigger function as follows:

```
warehouse_db=# CREATE OR REPLACE FUNCTION
                warehouse_audit_func_all()
RETURNS trigger AS $BODY$
BEGIN
--this IF block confirms the operation type to be INSERT.
  IF (TG_OP = 'INSERT') THEN
    INSERT INTO warehouse_audit
      (wlog_id, insertion_time, operation_detail)
    VALUES
      (new.warehouse_id, current_timestamp,'INSERT
      operation performed. Row with id '||NEW.warehouse_id||
      'inserted');
    RETURN NEW;
--this IF block confirms the operation type to be UPDATE.
  ELSIF (TG_OP = 'UPDATE') THEN
    INSERT INTO warehouse_audit
      (wlog_id, insertion_time, operation_detail)
    VALUES
      (NEW.warehouse_id, current_timestamp,'UPDATE operation
      performed. Row with id '||NEW.warehouse_id||' updates
      values '||OLD||' with '|| NEW.* ||'.');
    RETURN NEW;
--this IF block confirms the operation type to be DELETE
```

```
      ELSIF (TG_OP = 'DELETE') THEN
        INSERT INTO warehouse_audit
          (wlog_id, insertion_time, operation_detail)
        VALUES (OLD.warehouse_id, current_timestamp,'DELETE
          operation performed. Row with id '||OLD.warehouse_id||
          'deleted ');
        RETURN OLD;
      END IF;
      RETURN NULL;
    END;
    $BODY$ LANGUAGE plpgsql;
```

Now, we will create the trigger and bind it to the warehouse_tbl table as follows:

```
warehouse_db=# CREATE TRIGGER audit_all_ops_trigger
    AFTER INSERT OR UPDATE OR DELETE ON warehouse_tbl
    FOR EACH ROW
    EXECUTE PROCEDURE warehouse_audit_func_all();
```

Let's test our trigger by inserting, updating, and deleting rows from the warehouse_tbl table.

Insert rows in the warehouse_tbl table as follows:

```
warehouse_db=# INSERT INTO warehouse_tbl
  (warehouse_id, warehouse_name, year_created, street_address,
  city, state, zip)
VALUES
  (4, 'North point', 2011, 'Down Town', 'Carson', 'LA', 4324);

warehouse_db=# INSERT INTO warehouse_tbl
  (warehouse_id, warehouse_name, year_created, street_address,
  city, state, zip)
VALUES
  (5, 'South point', 2012, 'Down Town', 'Avalon', 'LA', 4325);
```

Update the city row in the warehouse_tbl table as follows:

```
warehouse_db=# UPDATE warehouse_tbl set city = 'arcadia' WHERE
                warehouse_id = '4';
```

Delete the row with warehouse_id as 4 in the warehouse_tbl table as follows:

```
warehouse_db=# DELETE FROM warehouse_tbl WHERE warehouse_id=4;
```

It's time to query the `warehouse_audit` table to see whether it recorded the changes we made on the `warehouse_tbl` table as follows:

```
warehouse_db=# SELECT wlog_id, insertion_time FROM
               warehouse_audit;
 wlog_id |          insertion_time
---------+-----------------------------
       4 | 2014-10-21 16:33:08.202+03
       5 | 2014-10-21 16:33:20.834+03
       4 | 2014-10-21 16:33:34.448+03
       4 | 2014-10-21 16:33:49.842+03
(4 rows)
```

Changes are successfully logged along with the type of the operation performed on the `warehouse_tbl` table.

Creating triggers on views

We said earlier that triggers can be attached to views as well. This example will demonstrate how to create triggers on views. We'll make use of a simple table called `tab_view` and a view called `view_select`.

First, create the `tab_view` table as follows:

```
warehouse_db=# CREATE TABLE tab_view
  (
  emp_id INT NOT NULL,
  emp_name VARCHAR(10),
  emp_city VARCHAR(10)
  );
```

Let's insert a few rows in the table in the following manner:

```
warehouse_db=# INSERT INTO tab_view VALUES (1, 'Adam', 'Chicago');
warehouse_db=# INSERT INTO tab_view VALUES (2, 'John', 'Miami');
warehouse_db=# INSERT INTO tab_view VALUES (3, 'Smith', 'Dallas');
```

Create the `view_select` view as follows:

```
warehouse_db=# CREATE VIEW view_select AS SELECT * FROM tab_view;
```

 Generally before PostgreSQL 9.3, if you try to update a view, it won't allow you to do so as views are *read only*, so you have to user triggers or rules to create such a mechanism. The latest versions of PostgreSQL 9.3 and onwards support the functionality of auto-updateable views.

We'll see how we can make an updateable view by creating a trigger as follows:

```
warehouse_db=# CREATE FUNCTION triggerfunc_on_view()
RETURNS trigger AS $$
BEGIN
  IF (TG_OP = 'INSERT') THEN
    INSERT INTO tab_view VALUES
    (NEW.emp_id, NEW.emp_name, NEW.emp_city);
    RETURN NEW;
  END IF;
  RETURN NULL;
END;
$$ LANGUAGE plpgsql;
```

Now, create a trigger and bind it to the view_select view as follows:

```
warehouse_db=# CREATE TRIGGER trigger_on_view
  INSTEAD OF INSERT ON view_select
  FOR EACH ROW
  EXECUTE PROCEDURE triggerfunc_on_view();
```

Let's check what view_select contains at this moment in the following manner:

```
warehouse_db=# SELECT * FROM view_select;
 emp_id | emp_name | emp_city
--------+----------+----------
      1 | Adam     | Chicago
      2 | John     | Miami
      3 | Smith    | Dallas
(3 rows)
```

Now, try to insert a row in the view_select view as follows:

```
warehouse_db=# INSERT INTO view_select VALUES
               (4, 'Gary', 'Houston');
```

Curious? Let's check the content of the table to see whether a row has been inserted in the following manner:

```
warehouse_db=# SELECT * FROM tab_view;
 emp_id | emp_name | emp_city
--------+----------+----------
      1 | Adam     | Chicago
      2 | John     | Miami
      3 | Smith    | Dallas
      4 | Gary     | Houston
(4 rows)
```

You can easily list the triggers you have created as follows:

```
warehouse_db=# SELECT * FROM pg_trigger;
```

The previous command will list all triggers but if you want to see triggers associated with a particular table, you can do that as well in the following manner:

```
warehouse_db=# SELECT tgname FROM pg_trigger, pg_class WHERE
                tgrelid=pg_class.oid AND relname='warehouse_tbl';
```

If you want to delete the triggers, use the DROP TRIGGER command as follows:

```
warehouse_db=# DROP TRIGGER audit_all_ops_trigger ON
                warehouse_tbl;
```

Creating triggers in PL/Perl

Triggers can be written in PL/Perl as well. You will be using the $_TD hash reference to access the information about a trigger event. $_TD is a global variable. The different fields of the $_TD hash reference are as follows:

- $_TD->{new}{col}: This is the NEW value of column
- $_TD->{old}{col}: This is the OLD value of column
- $_TD->{event}: This is the type of event, that is, whether it is INSERT, UPDATE, or DELETE
- $_TD->{table_name}: This is the name of table on which the trigger is fired

Let's create a simple trigger in PL/Perl. Before this, we will create a table called tab_perl, with three columns, emp_id, emp_name, and emp_city, as follows:

```
warehouse_db=# CREATE TABLE tab_perl
  (
  emp_id INT NOT NULL,
  emp_name VARCHAR(10),
  emp_city VARCHAR(10)
  );
```

It's always good to insert a few rows in the table to be tested. This is done as follows:

```
warehouse_db=# INSERT INTO tab_perl VALUES (1, 'Adam', 'Chicago');
warehouse_db=# INSERT INTO tab_perl VALUES (2, 'John', 'Miami');
```

We will now create a `perl_trigger_func` function that checks the values of `emp_id` before an `INSERT` operation. It will skip the operation if it is greater than or equal to `10`. If it is smaller than `10` it will insert the row:

```
warehouse_db=# CREATE EXTENSION plperl;
CREATE OR REPLACE FUNCTION perl_trigger_func()
RETURNS trigger AS $$
  IF ($_TD->{event} = 'INSERT') {
    IF (($_TD->{new}{emp_id} >= 10)) {
      RETURN "SKIP";}
    ELSE {
      RETURN; }
    }
$$ LANGUAGE plperl;
```

Now like all triggers, associate this with the table, `tab_perl` in this case. This is done in the following manner:

```
warehouse_db=# CREATE TRIGGER perl_trigger
  BEFORE INSERT ON tab_perl
  FOR EACH ROW
  EXECUTE PROCEDURE perl_trigger_func();
```

Now, try to insert a row with `emp_id` greater than `10` and check content of the table afterwards.

Insert the row in the `tab_perl` table using the following statement:

```
warehouse_db=# INSERT INTO tab_perl VALUES (13, 'Roger',
                'Boston');
```

Check the content of the table using the following statement:

```
warehouse_db=# SELECT * FROM tab_perl;
 emp_id | emp_name | emp_city
--------+----------+----------
      1 | Adam     | Chicago
      2 | John     | Miami
(2 rows)
```

So, `INSERT` is skipped. Now, let's add a row with `emp_id` smaller than `10` this time.

Insert the row in the `tab_perl` table using the following statement:

```
warehouse_db=# INSERT INTO tab_perl VALUES (3, 'Roger', 'Boston');
```

Check the table contents as follows:

```
warehouse_db=# SELECT * FROM tab_perl;
emp_id | emp_name | emp_city
--------+----------+----------
     1 | Adam     | Chicago
     2 | John     | Miami
     3 | Roger    | Boston
(3 rows)
```

This time the operation was successful and the table is updated.

Creating triggers in PL/Tcl

We will reuse the previous example to write trigger procedures in PL/Tcl. Let's go through the syntax for some of the trigger variables and give some information:

- $TG_name: This is the name of the trigger
- $TG_table_name: This is the name of the table to which the trigger is associated
- $TG_op: This is a string that can have the value INSERT, UPDATE, DELETE, or TRUNCATE
- $NEW: This is indexed by the column name; it's an associative array that contains new row values for INSERT, UPDATE, or empty in the case of DELETE
- $OLD: This is indexed by the column name; it's an associative array that contains old row values for UPDATE or DELETE or empty in the case of INSERT

Let's start with creating a table that contains a few rows in the following manner:

```
warehouse_db=# CREATE TABLE tab_tcl
  (
  emp_id INT NOT NULL,
  emp_name VARCHAR(10),
  emp_city VARCHAR(10)
  );
```

Insert rows in the tab_tcl table using the following statement:

```
warehouse_db=# INSERT INTO tab_tcl VALUES (1, 'Adam', 'Chicago');
warehouse_db=# INSERT INTO tab_tcl VALUES (2, 'John', 'Miami');
```

Create the PL/Tcl trigger function that will skip the INSERT operation if emp_id is greater than or equal to 10 and inserts it otherwise. This is done in the following manner:

```
warehouse_db=# CREATE EXTENSION pltcl;
CREATE FUNCTION tcl_trigger_func()
RETURNS trigger AS $$
  IF {$TG_op == "INSERT"} {
    IF { $NEW(emp_id) >= 10} {
      RETURN SKIP;}
  ELSE {
      RETURN OK;}
    }
$$ LANGUAGE pltcl;
```

Now, bind the trigger to the tab_tcl table in the following manner:

```
warehouse_db=# CREATE TRIGGER tcl_trigger
  BEFORE INSERT ON tab_tcl
  FOR EACH ROW
  EXECUTE PROCEDURE tcl_trigger_func();
```

We can now try to insert a row with emp_id greater than 10 and see what happens. The INSERT operation should not take place and should be skipped.

Insert a row in the tab_tcl table using the following statement:

```
warehouse_db=# INSERT INTO tab_tcl VALUES (13, 'Roger', 'Boston');
```

Check the content of the table using the following statement:

```
warehouse_db=# SELECT * FROM tab_tcl;
 emp_id | emp_name | emp_city
--------+----------+----------
      1 | Adam     | Chicago
      2 | John     | Miami
(2 rows)
```

Now, insert another row with emp_id smaller than 10 in the following manner (this time, the row will be inserted):

```
warehouse_db=# INSERT INTO tab_tcl VALUES (3, 'Roger', 'Boston');
```

We can retrieve values from the `tab_tcl` table using the SELECT command and check whether the row was indeed inserted in the following manner:

```
warehouse_db=# SELECT * FROM tab_tcl;
 emp_id | emp_name | emp_city
--------+----------+----------
      1 | Adam     | Chicago
      2 | John     | Miami
      3 | Roger    | Boston
(3 rows)
```

From the preceding output, we can see that the row was inserted in the `tbl_tcl` table.

Creating triggers in PL/Python

The PL/Python version of the previous example will be logically the same but syntactically different. You might have observed so far how trigger variables are accessed differently for all procedural languages. It will be good to see a few of them for PL/Python as well. They are as follows:

- `TD["name"]`: This is the name of the trigger
- `TD["table_name"]`: This is the name of the table to which the trigger is associated
- `TD["event"]`: This is a string that can have the value INSERT, UPDATE, DELETE, or TRUNCATE
- `TD["new"]`: This is the new trigger row for a row-level trigger
- `TD["old"]`: This is the old trigger row for a row-level trigger

We'll make use of the preceding variables in triggers ahead. Reuse the previous example to create and populate the sample table to bind the trigger later on.

Create the `tab_python` table in the following manner:

```
warehouse_db=# CREATE TABLE tab_python
  (
  emp_id INT NOT NULL,
  emp_name VARCHAR(10),
  emp_city VARCHAR(10)
  );
```

We will now insert two values in the `tab_python` table as follows:

```
warehouse_db=# INSERT INTO tab_python VALUES (1, 'Adam',
                'Chicago');
warehouse_db=# INSERT INTO tab_python VALUES (2, 'John', 'Miami');
```

Here goes the trigger function in Python. You'll be observing how the same logic is being used different syntactically. Returning SKIP will abort the transaction, which in this case is the INSERT operation:

```
warehouse_db=# CREATE EXTENSION plpython3u;
CREATE FUNCTION python_trigger_func()
RETURNS trigger AS $$
  IF TD["event"] == 'INSERT':
    IF TD["new"]["emp_id"] >= 10:
      RETURN "SKIP";
    RETURN "MODIFY"
$$ LANGUAGE plpython3u;
```

Finally, associate the trigger with the `tab_python` table:

```
warehouse_db=# CREATE TRIGGER python_trigger
  BEFORE INSERT ON tab_python
  FOR EACH ROW
  EXECUTE PROCEDURE python_trigger_func();
```

 Here, the indentation is significant in the Python language and if not handled well, can put you in trouble.

We'll try to insert rows with `emp_id` greater and smaller than `10` to see whether trigger is working:

```
warehouse_db=# INSERT INTO tab_python VALUES
                (13, 'Roger', 'Boston');
```

To check whether the row was inserted into the `tab_python` table, we will write a SELECT command as follows:

```
warehouse_db=# SELECT * FROM tab_python;
 emp_id | emp_name | emp_city
--------+----------+----------
      1 | Adam     | Chicago
      2 | John     | Miami
(2 rows)
```

We noticed that the INSERT operation was skipped and the row was not inserted.

Now, try inserting a row again into tab_python, but this time with a smaller emp_id using the following statement:

```
warehouse_db=# INSERT INTO tab_python VALUES (3, 'Roger',
                'Boston');
```

Now, check whether this time the row is inserted:

```
warehouse_db=# SELECT * FROM tab_python;
 emp_id | emp_name | emp_city
--------+----------+----------
      1 | Adam     | Chicago
      2 | John     | Miami
      3 | Roger    | Boston
(3 rows)
```

PostgreSQL rules

Things implemented through triggers can be achieved through rules as well. In fact, you can do more than this. To be concise, the PostgreSQL rule system is actually an implementation of query rewriting. The query rewrite module is located between the **parser** and the **planner**.

 Views in PostgreSQL are implemented using rules.

We will not go through an in-depth and tedious explanation of rules but it will be easy to skim through its basic concept.

Well, this is how the whole story begins and ends. A query is received by the server program and parsed by the parser that generates the **query tree** (it is an internal representation of an SQL statement). Before this query tree can be passed to the planner, the rules module rewrites the query tree with user-defined rewritten rules stored as a query tree in the catalog table pg_rewrite, the resultant output is another query tree for the planner that decides the optimal execution plan for the query.

 Rules should not reference a table that already has another associated rule set.

Rules versus triggers – creating updateable views with rules

In the various sections referring to triggers, we implemented updateable views using triggers; let's do it using rules. We are lucky that in the latest versions of PostgreSQL, we have auto-updateable views. We will use the same example where we implemented updateable views using triggers for the INSERT case.

Drop the tab_view table using the following statement:

```
warehouse_db=# DROP TABLE tab_view CASCADE;
```

Create the tab_view table again in the following manner:

```
warehouse_db=# CREATE TABLE tab_view
  (
  emp_id INT NOT NULL,
  emp_name VARCHAR(10),
  emp_city VARCHAR(10)
  );
```

Let's insert a few rows in the table in the following manner:

```
warehouse_db=# INSERT INTO tab_view VALUES (1, 'Adam', 'Chicago');
warehouse_db=# INSERT INTO tab_view VALUES (2, 'John', 'Miami');
warehouse_db=# INSERT INTO tab_view VALUES (3, 'Smith', 'Dallas');
```

Create the view_select view using the following statement:

```
warehouse_db=# CREATE VIEW view_select AS SELECT * FROM tab_view;
```

Create the rule for INSERT on the view in the following manner:

```
warehouse_db=# CREATE RULE view_select_insert AS ON INSERT
  TO view_select
  DO INSTEAD (INSERT INTO tab_view VALUES
  (NEW.emp_id, NEW.emp_name, NEW.emp_city));
```

You can list your rule by querying the pg_rewrite catalog table to see whether your rule has been created in the following manner:

```
warehouse_db=# SELECT rulename FROM pg_rewrite WHERE
              rulename='view_select_insert';
      rulename
-------------------
 view_select_insert
(1 row)
```

Now, insert a row in the `view_select` view using the following statement:

```
warehouse_db=# INSERT INTO view_select VALUES
                (4, 'Gary', 'Houston');
```

Use the `SELECT` command to check whether the changes are logged in the view as follows:

```
warehouse_db=# SELECT * FROM tab_view;
 emp_id | emp_name | emp_city
--------+----------+----------
      1 | Adam     | Chicago
      2 | John     | Miami
      3 | Smith    | Dallas
      4 | Gary     | Houston
(4 rows)
```

You have successfully created an updateable view using rules.

Triggers are fired for each affected row and procedural whereas rules modify the query tree, and for a database, it's a pure SQL statement. Thus, all rows will be affected at once. This feature makes them faster as compared to triggers. This difference would not be evident if you are affecting merely few rows. However, as the complexity grows, maintaining rules will become difficult whereas in triggers, complexity is quite low. So, the choice between rules and triggers is certainly related to the usage and level of complexities involved.

Understanding views

Though the name view itself hints at an object that lets you view, and in databases, we mean a database object that helps you view the table data. It's not a real table itself but can serve as a *read-only* view of the table you have associated with. Unlike tables, views do not exist on their own. They are helpful in the following ways:

- They are created on the table as a query to select all or selective columns, thus giving restricted or privileged access. Accessing actual data is not at all required.

- They are capable of joining multiple tables to represent data as a single table.

- They are not real, thus they only use storage space for definition and not for the actual data they collect.

- They always bring the updated data when accessed.

Prior to the concept of **auto-updatable views** in PostgreSQL, one could not perform an INSERT, UPDATE, or DELETE operation on views and used rules or triggers to make this happen.

Databases are understood well with hands-on experience. We will first write a code for a simple view that will collect data from the warehouse_tbl table. Moving forward, we will join two tables to see how it works.

As per the PostgreSQL manual, here is the general syntax to create a view:

```
CREATE [ OR REPLACE ] [ TEMP | TEMPORARY ] [ RECURSIVE ] VIEW name
  [ ( column_name [, ...] ) ]
  [ WITH ( view_option_name [= view_option_value] [, ... ] ) ]
  AS query
  [ WITH [ CASCADED | LOCAL ] CHECK OPTION ]
```

Now, proceed to actually create a view, which is as easy as creating a table, using the following statement:

```
warehouse_db=# CREATE VIEW view_warehouse_tbl
  AS SELECT *
  FROM warehouse_tbl;
```

The preceding statement has created a view called view_warehouse_tbl in the form of a SELECT query. You can access this view to see the results using the following statement:

```
warehouse_db=# SELECT warehouse_id, warehouse_name, state FROM
                view_warehouse_tbl;
 warehouse_id | warehouse_name | state
--------------+----------------+-------
            1 | Mark Corp      | CT
            2 | Bill & Co      | CT
            3 | West point     | CT
            5 | South point    | LA
(4 rows)
```

Now, suppose your database design is required not to permit access to tables directly but to give a restricted access to viewing the table data. For this, you should create a view that joins multiple tables with selective columns.

The `warehouse_tbl` and `history` tables have many columns but you are interested only in showing a few columns to the users. These columns are:

- The `warehouse_name`, `year_created`, and `city` columns from the `warehouse_tbl` table
- The `amount` and `date` columns from the `history` table

You will create a view that is created on multiple tables as a `SELECT` query and display data as one table. Here, `view_multiple_tables` first selects columns to be shown from both tables and then validates the IDs in the `WHERE` clause.

Create a view on the multiple tables in the following manner:

```
warehouse_db=# CREATE VIEW view_multiple_tables
  AS SELECT warehouse_name, year_created, city, amount, date
  FROM record.warehouse_tbl, record.history
  WHERE warehouse_tbl.warehouse_id = history.warehouse_id;
```

Now, perform a `SELECT` query to see the content of the view:

```
warehouse_db=# SELECT * FROM view_multiple_tables;
```

Insert a few rows in both tables and access the view again to see whether it refreshes the data. The first `INSERT` statement inserts data into the `warehouse_tbl` table and the next `INSERT` statement inserts data in the `history` table.

Insert rows in both tables as follows:

```
warehouse_db=# INSERT INTO warehouse_tbl
  (warehouse_id, warehouse_name, year_created, street_address,
  city, state, zip)
VALUES
  (6, 'Jackson & Co', 2010, 'lincoln Road', 'Buffalo', 'NY',
  4331);

warehouse_db=# INSERT INTO history
  (history_id, date, amount, data, customer_id, warehouse_id)
VALUES
  (1, 'Jul-10-14', 1234, 'thedata', 1, 1);

warehouse_db=# INSERT INTO history
  (history_id, date, amount, data, customer_id, warehouse_id)
VALUES
  (2, 'Jul-10-15', 2345, 'thedatasecond', 2, 2);
```

To check whether the `INSERT` operation affects our view and reflects the updated tables, we will use a `SELECT` command as follows:

```
warehouse_db=# SELECT * FROM view_multiple_tables;
 warehouse_name | year_created |    city     | amount |    date
----------------+--------------+-------------+--------+-----------
 Mark Corp      |         2009 | New London  |   1234 | 2014-07-10
                |              |             |        | 00:00:00
 Bill & Co      |         2014 | New London  |   2345 | 2015-07-10
                |              |             |        | 00:00:00
(2 rows)
```

You can list your views as well that you just created by the `\dv` command in the `psql` utility as follows:

```
warehouse_db=# \dv
                List of relations
 Schema |         Name          | Type |   Owner
--------+-----------------------+------+----------
 record | view_multiple_tables  | view | postgres
 record | view_warehouse_tbl    | view | postgres
(2 rows)
```

Dropping the view is also a simple process like dropping a table. This can be done using the following statement:

```
warehouse_db=# DROP VIEW view_warehouse_tbl;
```

You can see how easy it was to create views and empower your database design.

Materialized views

We said views are read only and the logical representation of data that is not stored on disk or database. Views can be materialized in a way that they can still be a logical representation of the data but when stored physically on the disk, at that moment they become **materialized views**.

You will quickly jump to ask, "Why not stick to tables then?" Well, materialized views have proved their capacity to work when performance is required, that is, when there are more reads than writes. Materialized view data will be stored in a table that can be indexed quickly when joining and that too has to be done when you have to refresh the materialized views.

Thus, when your query has to bring millions of rows and querying the actual database through views is expensive, you will definitely like to have queries (views) that are stored physically such as tables and give quick response. This is the reason materialized views are used in data warehouses and Business Intelligence applications.

Creating materialized views

Creating a materialized view is slightly different to regular views but populating it is entirely different and requires a different mechanism. Unlike regular views that bring the updated data, materialized views gets populated depending on how you created them and you need a refresh mechanism to do this. Its syntax is as follows:

```
warehouse_db=# CREATE MATERIALIZED VIEW record.mat_view
  AS SELECT * FROM warehouse_tbl
  WITH NO DATA;
```

> Using `WITH NO DATA` will decide whether a view should be populated at creation time or not. If you opt `WITH NO DATA`, the materialized view will cannot be queried until `REFRESH MATERIALIZED VIEW` is used.

We'll insert a few rows and try to access a materialized view as follows:

```
warehouse_db=# INSERT INTO warehouse_tbl
  (warehouse_id, warehouse_name, year_created, street_address,
  city, state, zip)
VALUES
  (7, 'GMC', 2011, 'getsby Road', 'Fulton', 'NY', 4332);


warehouse_db=# INSERT INTO warehouse_tbl
  (warehouse_id, warehouse_name, year_created, street_address,
  city, state, zip)
VALUES
  (8, 'Ford', 2012, 'fisa Road', 'Elmira', 'NY', 4333);
```

Now, use a `SELECT` command to check whether the records have been inserted successfully as follows:

```
warehouse_db=# SELECT * FROM record.mat_view;
ERROR:  materialized view "mat_view" has not been populated
HINT:  Use the REFRESH MATERIALIZED VIEW command.
```

Execute the following command to resolve the preceding error:

```
warehouse_db=# REFRESH MATERIALIZED VIEW record.mat_view;
```

In PostgreSQL 9.4, you can query a materialized view while it's being refreshed for new data from the parent table. Earlier versions prevented querying, as refreshing acquires a lock. This can be done with the `CONCURRENTLY` keyword as follows:

```
warehouse_db=# REFRESH MATERIALIZED VIEW CONCURRENTLY mat_view;
```

For this, a unique index is required to exist on a materialized view. Now, executing a SELECT command will bring the updated records:

```
warehouse_db=# SELECT warehouse_id, warehouse_name, city, state
            FROM record.mat_view;
 warehouse_id | warehouse_name |    city     | state
--------------+----------------+-------------+-------
            1 | Mark Corp      | New London  | CT
            2 | Bill & Co      | New London  | CT
            3 | West point     | New London  | CT
            5 | South point    | Avalon      | LA
            6 | Jackson & Co   | Buffalo     | NY
            7 | GMC            | Fulton      | NY
            8 | Ford           | Elmira      | NY
(7 rows)
```

Dropping a materialized view is pretty straightforward as we have done for tables and views. This is done using the following statement:

```
warehouse_db=# DROP MATERIALIZED VIEW record.mat_view;
```

There is much to explore after learning the power of triggers and views. This will work when you are actually playing with them and can work wonders with regular practice.

Summary

Learning PostgreSQL concepts will surely help you advance your skillsets to a higher level. After going through this chapter, you have acquainted yourself with the concepts of triggers, rules, and views. You have learned the underlying concepts of their usage and efficiency they bring along. Implementing triggers in native PostgreSQL languages is a plus. You have got a glimpse of PostgreSQL rules as well. If you are passionate to learn more, then the next topic that you will see is window functions.

5
Window Functions

Window functions are built-in functions provided by PostgreSQL. They are used for calculation between multiple rows, which are related to the current query row.

Let's start to play around with the various window functions.

In this chapter, we will discuss the following topics:

- How the window functions are in conjunction with the aggregate functions
- The scope, structure, and usage of the window functions with examples
- What each window function is for

Understanding window functions

Window functions are used to perform advance sorting and limit the number of rows returned on a subset of a joined table of data. We will look at `cume_dist()`, `row_number()`, `rank()`, `dense_rank()`, `present_rank()`, `first_value()`, `last_value()`, `nth_value()`, `ntile()`, `lag()` and `lead()` built-in window functions. User-defined aggregate functions can also act as window functions by calling the `OVER` keyword. In this chapter, you will learn only about the PostgreSQL built-in window function.

We have 11 window functions; we will see each of the 11 functions in the following sections.

The cume_dist() function

The `cume_dist()` function is used to get the relative rank of the current row. It is calculated by dividing the number of rows preceding the current row by the total number of rows. This can be seen by the following formula:

Rank of current row = Number of rows preceding the current row / total number of rows

Consider the `warehouse_departments` table that has data, as shown here:

```
warehouse_db=# SELECT * FROM warehouse_departments
 department_no | department_name | department_location
---------------+-----------------+--------------------
            10 | ACCOUNTING      | NEW YORK
            20 | RESEARCH        | DALLAS
            30 | SALES           | CHICAGO
            40 | OPERATIONS      | BOSTON
            30 | SALES_OUTER     | CHICAGO
            30 | SALES_INSIDE    | CHICAGO
            20 | RESEARCH_OPEN   | PARIS
(7 rows)
```

Let's call the `cume_dist()` function to see what we actually have in the results using the following statement:

```
warehouse_db=# SELECT department_no, department_name,
               department_location,cume_dist() OVER (ORDER BY
               department_no) FROM warehouse_departments;
 department_no | department_name | department_location | cume_dist
---------------+-----------------+---------------------+----------
            10 | ACCOUNTING      | NEW YORK            |      0.14
            20 | RESEARCH_OPEN   | PARIS               |      0.42
            20 | RESEARCH        | DALLAS              |      0.42
            30 | SALES           | CHICAGO             |      0.85
            30 | SALES_OUTER     | CHICAGO             |      0.85
            30 | SALES_INSIDE    | CHICAGO             |      0.85
            40 | OPERATIONS      | BOSTON              |         1
(7 rows)
```

As we used the OVER clause on department number, the `cume_dist()` function will assign the same rank to departments that have the same department number.

The results show that:

- The rank of the first row with department number 10 is *1/7 = 0.14*

- The rank of the second and third rows with department number 20 is *3/7 = 0.42*

- The rank of the fourth, fifth, and sixth rows is *6/7 = 0.85*

- The rank of the seventh row is *7/7 = 1*

The row_number() function

The row_number() function is used to get the number of the current row within its partition, starting from 1. Let's call the row_number() function using the following statement and see the results we get:

```
warehouse_db=# SELECT department_no, department_name,
          department_location, row_number() OVER (PARTITION
          BY department_no) FROM warehouse_departments;
 department_no | department_name | department_location | row_number
---------------+-----------------+---------------------+------------
            10 | ACCOUNTING      | NEW YORK            |          1
            20 | RESEARCH_OPEN   | PARIS               |          1
            20 | RESEARCH        | DALLAS              |          2
            30 | SALES           | CHICAGO             |          1
            30 | SALES_OUTER     | CHICAGO             |          2
            30 | SALES_INSIDE    | CHICAGO             |          3
            40 | OPERATIONS      | BOSTON              |          1
(7 rows)
```

The result of the table shows the number of rows based on the department number partition, which can be explained in the following manner:

- The department number 10 has only one row with row_number 1

- The department number 20 has two rows starting from number 1 up to number 2

- The department number 30 has three rows starting from number 1 up to number 3

- The department number 40 has only one row with row_number 1

The rank() function

The `rank()` function is used to get the ranks of the current row with a gap. Let's call the `rank()` function to see what we have as results:

```
warehouse_db=# SELECT department_no, department_name,
               department_location, rank() OVER (PARTITION BY
               department_no ORDER BY department_name) FROM
               warehouse_departments;
```

department_no	department_name	department_location	rank
10	ACCOUNTING	NEW YORK	1
20	RESEARCH	DALLAS	1
20	RESEARCH_OPEN	PARIS	2
30	SALES	CHICAGO	1
30	SALES_INSIDE	CHICAGO	2
30	SALES_OUTER	CHICAGO	3
40	OPERATIONS	BOSTON	1

(7 rows)

The previous statement ranks the departments based on department name. This can be explained as follows:

- The department number 10 got rank 1 based on department name, that is, ACCOUNTING

- The department number 20 got rank 1 and 2 based on department name, that is, RESEARCH and RESEARCH_OPEN

- The department number 30 got rank 1, 2, and 3 based on three different department names, that is, SALES, SALES_INSIDE, and SALES_OUTER

- The department number 40 got rank 1 based on department name, that is, OPERATIONS

Consider the following statement that ranks the departments based on the department location. In the current case, records having the same department location value will get the same rank.

```
warehouse_db=# SELECT department_no, department_name,
               department_location, rank() OVER (ORDER BY
               department_location) FROM warehouse_departments;
```

department_no	department_name	department_location	rank
40	OPERATIONS	BOSTON	1
30	SALES	CHICAGO	2
30	SALES_OUTER	CHICAGO	2
30	SALES_INSIDE	CHICAGO	2

```
           20 | RESEARCH       | DALLAS        |      5
           10 | ACCOUNTING     | NEW YORK      |      6
           20 | RESEARCH_OPEN  | PARIS         |      7
(7 rows)
```

The dense_rank() function

The `dense_rank()` function is used to get the rank of the current row without any gaps. Rows with equal values for the ranking criteria receive the same rank. The `dense_rank()` function differs from the `rank()` function in one respect; if there is a tie between two or more rows, there is no gap in the sequence of the ranked values. Let's call the `dense_rank()` function to see the results:

```
warehouse_db=# SELECT department_no, department_name,
               department_location, dense_rank() OVER (order by
               department_no) FROM warehouse_departments;
department_no | department_name | department_location | dense_rank
--------------+-----------------+---------------------+-----------
           10 | ACCOUNTING      | NEW YORK            |      1
           20 | RESEARCH_OPEN   | PARIS               |      2
           20 | RESEARCH        | DALLAS              |      2
           30 | SALES           | CHICAGO             |      3
           30 | SALES_OUTER     | CHICAGO             |      3
           30 | SALES_INSIDE    | CHICAGO             |      3
           40 | OPERATIONS      | BOSTON              |      4
(7 rows)
```

We have four different types of department number. So, the maximum rank is 4 and the results show that:

- The row with department number 10 has `dense_rank` 1
- The `dense_rank` value of `row_number` 2 and 3 with department number 20 is 2
- The `dense_rank` value of `row_number` 4, 5, and 6 with department number 30 is 3
- The `dense_rank` value of `row_number` 7 with department number 40 is 4

If we use department_name in the OVER clause, we will have different ranks, as shown in the following output, because we have all distinct department names:

```
warehouse_db=# SELECT department_no, department_name,
               department_location, dense_rank() OVER (ORDER BY
               department_name) FROM warehouse_departments;
 department_no | department_name | department_location | dense_rank
---------------+-----------------+---------------------+------------
            10 | ACCOUNTING      | NEW YORK            |          1
            40 | OPERATIONS      | BOSTON              |          2
            20 | RESEARCH        | DALLAS              |          3
            20 | RESEARCH_OPEN   | PARIS               |          4
            30 | SALES           | CHICAGO             |          5
            30 | SALES_INSIDE    | CHICAGO             |          6
            30 | SALES_OUTER     | CHICAGO             |          7
(7 rows)
```

The percent_rank() function

The percent_rank() function is used to get the relative rank of the current row. The relative rank of the current row is calculated using the following formula:

Relative rank of the current row = (rank - 1) / (total number of rows - 1)

Let's understand this with the following example:

```
warehouse_db=# SELECT department_no, department_name,
               department_location, percent_rank() OVER (PARTITION
               BY department_no ORDER BY department_name) FROM
               warehouse_departments;
 department_no | department_name | department_location | percent_rank
---------------+-----------------+---------------------+--------------
            10 | ACCOUNTING      | NEW YORK            |            0
            20 | RESEARCH        | DALLAS              |            0
            20 | RESEARCH_OPEN   | PARIS               |            1
            30 | SALES           | CHICAGO             |            0
            30 | SALES_INSIDE    | CHICAGO             |          0.5
            30 | SALES_OUTER     | CHICAGO             |            1
            40 | OPERATIONS      | BOSTON              |            0
(7 rows)
```

We used the PARTITION BY clause on department_no, so percent_rank will be within the same department number. This can be explained in the following manner:

- The department number 10 has percent_rank 0

- The department number 20 has percent_rank 0 and 1

- The department number 30 has percent_rank 0, 0.5, and 1

- The department number 40 has percent_rank 1, and it is calculated using the preceding relative rank equation

The first_value() function

The first_value() function is used to get a value evaluated at the first row of the window frame. The first_value() function takes the column name as the input argument. Let's understand this with the following example:

```
warehouse_db=# SELECT department_no, department_name,
        department_location, first_value(department_no)
        OVER (ORDER BY department_no) FROM
        warehouse_departments WHERE department_no > 20;
 department_no | department_name | department_location | first_value
---------------+-----------------+---------------------+------------
            30 | SALES           | CHICAGO             |          30
            30 | SALES_OUTER     | CHICAGO             |          30
            30 | SALES_INSIDE    | CHICAGO             |          30
            40 | OPERATIONS      | BOSTON              |          30
(4 rows)
```

In the preceding example, we get the records where department_no is greater than 20, and we applied the ORDER BY clause on department_no. So in return, we will get the list of records that have department_no greater than 20. The first department number is 30, so this is why the first_value() function returns 30.

Let's see another example, and this time, we are sorting the records by department location. As a result, Boston is the first row. The value of department_no is 40, so this is why we get first_value as 40. This is shown in the following code:

```
warehouse_db=# SELECT department_no, department_name,
        department_location, first_value(department_no)
        OVER (ORDER BY department_location) FROM
        warehouse_departments WHERE department_no >20;
 department_no | department_name | department_location | first_value
```

```
-------------+----------------+---------------------+-----------
       40 | OPERATIONS     | BOSTON              |        40
       30 | SALES          | CHICAGO             |        40
       30 | SALES_OUTER    | CHICAGO             |        40
       30 | SALES_INSIDE   | CHICAGO             |        40
(4 rows)
```

The last_value() function

The last_value() function is used to get the value evaluated at the last row of the window frame. The last_value() function takes the column name as the input argument. Let's understand this with the following example:

```
warehouse_db=# SELECT department_no, department_name,
               department_location, last_value(department_no) OVER
               (ORDER BY department_name) FROM
               warehouse_departments;
 department_no | department_name | department_location | last_value
---------------+-----------------+---------------------+-----------
        10 | ACCOUNTING      | NEW YORK            |        10
        40 | OPERATIONS      | BOSTON              |        40
        20 | RESEARCH        | DALLAS              |        20
        20 | RESEARCH_OPEN   | PARIS               |        20
        30 | SALES           | CHICAGO             |        30
        30 | SALES_INSIDE    | CHICAGO             |        30
        30 | SALES_OUTER     | CHICAGO             |        30
(7 rows)
```

The last record that we get on the basis of the ORDER BY clause in department_name is SALES_OUTER with the value of department_no equal to 30. Hence, the value of last_value is 30.

The nth_value() function

The nth_value() function is used to get a value evaluated at the row that is the nth row of the window frame. The nth_value() function takes the column name and nth number as the input argument. It returns the null value if the nth value is not present in the table. Let's understand this with the following example:

```
warehouse_db=# SELECT department_no, department_name,
               department_location,
               nth_value(department_location,2) OVER (PARTITION BY
               department_no ORDER BY department_name) FROM
               warehouse_departments;
```

```
 department_no | department_name | department_location | nth_value
---------------+-----------------+----------------------+----------
            10 | ACCOUNTING      | NEW YORK             |
            20 | RESEARCH        | DALLAS               |
            20 | RESEARCH_OPEN   | PARIS                | PARIS
            30 | SALES           | CHICAGO              |
            30 | SALES_INSIDE    | CHICAGO              | CHICAGO
            30 | SALES_OUTER     | CHICAGO              | CHICAGO
            40 | OPERATIONS      | BOSTON               |
(7 rows)
```

In the preceding example, we used the PARTITION BY clause and partitioned the records based on department number, so in every partition, the nth number (in our case, we give 2) will be the output of the nth_value function. This can be explained in the following manner:

- The department number 10 only has one row and no second row, so the nth value is null

- The department number 20 has two rows and the second row has department_location as PARIS

- The department number 30 has three rows and the second row has department_location as CHICAGO

- The department number 40 has one row and no second row, so the nth value is null

The ntile() function

The ntile() function returns an integer ranging from 1 to the argument value, divides the partition as equally as possible, and assigns an appropriate bucket number to each row. Let's understand this with the following example:

```
warehouse_db=# SELECT department_no, department_name,
               department_location, ntile(2) OVER (ORDER BY
               department_no) FROM warehouse_departments;
 department_no | department_name | department_location | ntile
---------------+-----------------+----------------------+-------
            10 | ACCOUNTING      | NEW YORK             |     1
            20 | RESEARCH_OPEN   | PARIS                |     1
            20 | RESEARCH        | DALLAS               |     1
            30 | SALES           | CHICAGO              |     1
            30 | SALES_OUTER     | CHICAGO              |     2
            30 | SALES_INSIDE    | CHICAGO              |     2
            40 | OPERATIONS      | BOSTON               |     2
(7 rows)
```

In the preceding example, the table is divided into two partitions by the `ntile()` function.

Let's call the function again, give 3 as the argument to the `ntile()` function, and see the impact on the results as follows:

```
warehouse_db=# SELECT department_no, department_name,
              department_location, ntile(3) OVER (ORDER BY
              department_no) FROM warehouse_departments;
 department_no | department_name | department_location | ntile
---------------+-----------------+---------------------+-------
            10 | ACCOUNTING      | NEW YORK            |     1
            20 | RESEARCH_OPEN   | PARIS               |     1
            20 | RESEARCH        | DALLAS              |     1
            30 | SALES           | CHICAGO             |     2
            30 | SALES_OUTER     | CHICAGO             |     2
            30 | SALES_INSIDE    | CHICAGO             |     3
            40 | OPERATIONS      | BOSTON              |     3
(7 rows)
```

In the preceding example, the table is divided into three partitions by the `ntile()` function.

The lag() function

The `lag()` function is used to access more than one row of a table at the same time without using a **self join**. Considering that the number of rows returned from a query and the position of the cursor, `lag()` gives direction to a row at a given physical offset prior to that position. To understand this functionality in detail, let's try to actually use this in our query:

```
warehouse_db=# SELECT department_no, department_name,
              department_location, lag(department_no,3) OVER
              (ORDER BY department_no) FROM
              warehouse_departments;
 department_no | department_name | department_location | lag
---------------+-----------------+---------------------+-----
            10 | ACCOUNTING      | NEW YORK            |
            20 | RESEARCH_OPEN   | PARIS               |
            20 | RESEARCH        | DALLAS              |
            30 | SALES           | CHICAGO             |  10
            30 | SALES_OUTER     | CHICAGO             |  20
            30 | SALES_INSIDE    | CHICAGO             |  20
            40 | OPERATIONS      | BOSTON              |  30
(7 rows)
```

In the preceding example, we give three arguments to the `lag()` function. The first is the column name on the basis of which the `lag()` function will access `department_no`. The second argument is an offset value, which in our case is `3`, and this means that the cursor will start from the fourth value and make a self join of `department_no` with the remaining record.

The lead() function

The `lead()` function is used to get the evaluated values of rows that are offset rows after the current row within the partition. If the offset argument is not given at the time of calling the function, it is set to `1` by default.

Let's understand this with the following example. In this example, we partition a table on the base of `department_no` and then call the `lead()` function for `department_name` with an offset value equal to `1`; this will result in the following output:

```
warehouse_db=# SELECT department_no, department_name,
               department_location, lead(department_name,1) OVER
               (PARTITION BY department_no ORDER BY department_no)
               FROM warehouse_departments;
 department_no | department_name | department_location |    lead
---------------+-----------------+---------------------+-------------
            10 | ACCOUNTING      | NEW YORK            |
            20 | RESEARCH_OPEN   | PARIS               | RESEARCH
            20 | RESEARCH        | DALLAS              |
            30 | SALES           | CHICAGO             |SALES_OUTER
            30 | SALES_OUTER     | CHICAGO             |SALES_INSIDE
            30 | SALES_INSIDE    | CHICAGO             |
            40 | OPERATIONS      | BOSTON              |
(7 rows)
```

The preceding example has the following results:

- The department number `10` has only one row, so there is no `lead` value as the offset is `1`

- The department number `20` has two rows and has `RESEARCH` as `lead`

- The department number `30` has three rows; the first row is skipped as offset is `1` and the remaining rows have `SALES_OUTER` and `SALES_INSIDE` as `lead`

- The department number `40` has only one row, so no `lead` value as offset is `1`

Summary

In this chapter, you learned the `cume_dist`, `row_number`, `rank`, `dense_rank`, `percent_rank`, `first_value`, `last_value`, `nth_value`, `ntile`, `lag` and `lead` window functions. You also learned their usage in PostgreSQL. We used the window functions to perform advance sorting and limiting on a subset of a joined table of data. We also learned that we can use window functions when we need more complex sorting or limiting behavior. Hope you enjoyed all that you learned in this chapter. If you want to know more about window functions, you can explore more about them at the following link:

`http://www.postgresql.org/docs/9.4/static/tutorial-window.html`.

In the next chapter, you will learn about table partitioning in detail.

6
Partitioning

The process of dividing the tables into smaller manageable parts is called **partitioning**, and these smaller manageable parts are called **partitions**.

In the process of partitioning, we divide one logical big table into multiple physical smaller parts.

Before actually creating the partitions, let's understand why we need partitions. The first and most demanding reason to use partitions in a database is to increase the performance of the database. This is achieved by partition-wise joins; if a user's queries perform a lot of full-table scans, partitioning will help vastly, because partitions will limit the scope of this search. The second important reason to partition is ease of managing large tables.

Partitioning always helps manage large objects. Although it is applicable to objects of any size, the advantages are more apparent in large tables. When a user recreates an index on a nonpartitioned table, the only option is to build the entire index in one statement. On the other hand, if the table is partitioned, the user can rebuild partitions of the local indexes one at a time.

In this chapter, we will learn the following topics:

- Why we need partitions
- Different types of partitions in PostgreSQL

Creating a table partition

PostgreSQL supports table partitioning through table inheritance, which means every partition will be created as a child table of a single parent table. Partitioning is performed in such a way that every child table inherits a single parent table. The parent table will be empty; it exists just to describe the whole dataset. Currently in PostgreSQL, partitioning can be implemented in **range partitioning** or **list partitioning**.

Partitioning in PostgreSQL

Range partitioning can be done, for example, by record number ranges (such as record 0 to 100 or 100 to 200) or even using date ranges (such as from 2014-11-01 to 2014-11-30).

List partitioning can be done, for example, by a list of cities (such as New York, Boston, Chicago, and Houston) or list of departments (such as HR, finance, administration, and so on). We will use multiple examples so that you are familiar with both of these types.

There are five simple steps used to create a partition in PostgreSQL, which are as follows:

1. Create the master table.
2. Create multiple child tables without having an overlapped table constraint.
3. Create indexes.
4. Create a trigger function to insert data into child tables.
5. Enable the constraint exclusion.

Range partition

The range partition is the partition in which we partition a table into ranges defined by a single column or multiple columns. When defining the ranges, the user will have to take care that ranges should be connected and not overlapping with each other; moreover, ranges must be defined using the < value operator. For instance, one can partition by date ranges or ranges of identifiers for specific business objects. To illustrate the range partition, we are going to create a table that contains the sales-related record for the year 2014.

Creating the master table

So, let's start by creating a simple master table. This table will contain data on sales stored on a daily basis. This will be done in the following manner:

```
warehouse_db=# CREATE TABLE sales_record
  (
  id NUMERIC PRIMARY KEY,
  sales_amount NUMERIC,
  sales_date DATE NOT NULL DEFAULT CURRENT_DATE
  );
```

This is the parent table; all the records that a user inserts in this table will move to the child table based on the criteria of `sales_date` that we are going to create in the following section.

Creating a range partition table

To implement the partition, we will create child tables. All child tables will inherit the master table. We will add the CHECK constraint for dates because we want to make sure that we have only the correct data on each partition. Partitions starts from the date `2014-01-01` and end on the date `2014-12-31`. Each partition will have two months' data.

Create the `sales_record_m1_to_m2` child table as follows:

```
warehouse_db=# CREATE TABLE sales_record_m1_to_m2
  (
  PRIMARY KEY (id, sales_date),
  CHECK (sales_date >= DATE '2014-01-01'
  AND sales_date < DATE '2014-03-01')
  )
  INHERITS (sales_record);
```

This child table will contain data of January and February.

Now, create the `sales_record_m3_to_m4` child table as follows:

```
warehouse_db=# CREATE TABLE sales_record_m3_to_m4
  (
  PRIMARY KEY (id, sales_date),
  CHECK (sales_date >= DATE '2014-03-01'
  AND sales_date < DATE '2014-05-01')
  )
  INHERITS (sales_record);
```

This child table will contain data of March and April.

Create the `sales_record_m5_to_m6` child table as follows:

```
warehouse_db=# CREATE TABLE sales_record_m5_to_m6
  (
  PRIMARY KEY (id, sales_date),
  CHECK (sales_date >= DATE '2014-05-01'
  AND sales_date < DATE '2014-07-01')
  )
  INHERITS (sales_record);
```

This child table will contain data of May and June.

Create the `sales_record_m7_to_m8` child table as follows:

```
warehouse_db=# CREATE TABLE sales_record_m7_to_m8
  (
  PRIMARY KEY (id, sales_date),
  CHECK (sales_date >= DATE '2014-07-01'
  AND sales_date < DATE '2014-09-01')
  )
  INHERITS (sales_record);
```

This child table will contain data of July and August.

Create the `sales_record_m9_to_m10` child table as follows:

```
warehouse_db=# CREATE TABLE sales_record_m9_to_m10
  (
  PRIMARY KEY (id, sales_date),
  CHECK (sales_date >= DATE '2014-09-01'
  AND sales_date < DATE '2014-11-01')
  )
  INHERITS (sales_record);
```

This child table will contain data of September and October.

Now, create the `sales_record_m11_to_m12` child table as follows:

```
warehouse_db=# CREATE TABLE sales_record_m11_to_m12
  (
  PRIMARY KEY (id, sales_date),
  CHECK (sales_date >= DATE '2014-11-01'
  AND sales_date < DATE '2015-01-01')
  )
  INHERITS (sales_record);
```

This child table will contain data of November and December.

 You can verify that the tables are linked and the partition is successfully created using the following query:
```
warehouse_db=# \d+ sales_record
```

Creating an index on child tables

Until now, we have created the master table and child tables inherited from the master table. Now, we are going to create indexes on child tables to speed up the sales_day field usage, using almost all queries (INSERT, SELECT, and UPDATE) on the date field.

Create the m1_to_m2_sales_date index on the sales_record_m1_to_m2 child table as follows:

```
warehouse_db=# CREATE INDEX m1_to_m2_sales_date ON
                    sales_record_m1_to_m2 (sales_date);
```

Create the m3_to_m4_sales_date index on the sales_record_m3_to_m4 child table as follows:

```
warehouse_db=# CREATE INDEX m3_to_m4_sales_date ON
                    sales_record_m3_to_m4 (sales_date);
```

Now, let's create the m5_to_m6_sales_date index on the sales_record_m5_to_m6 child table:

```
warehouse_db=# CREATE INDEX m5_to_m6_sales_date ON
                    sales_record_m5_to_m6 (sales_date);
```

Create the m7_to_m8_sales_date index on the sales_record_m7_to_m8 child table as follows:

```
warehouse_db=# CREATE INDEX m7_to_m8_sales_date ON
                    sales_record_m7_to_m8 (sales_date);
```

Then, create the m9_to_m10_sales_date index on the sales_record_m9_to_m10 child table as follows:

```
warehouse_db=# CREATE INDEX m9_to_m10_sales_date ON
                    sales_record_m9_to_m10 (sales_date);
```

Create the m11_to_m12_sales_date index on the sales_record_m11_to_m12 child table as follows:

```
warehouse_db=# CREATE INDEX m11_to_m12_sales_date ON
                    sales_record_m11_to_m12 (sales_date);
```

Creating a trigger on the master table

The next thing that we need after the indexes is to create a trigger and the trigger function to the master table. Conditions must be exactly the same as what the child tables check.

So, let's first create a trigger function using the following syntax:

```
warehouse_db=# CREATE OR REPLACE FUNCTION sales_record_insert()
RETURNS TRIGGER AS $$
BEGIN
  IF (NEW.sales_date >= DATE '2014-01-01' AND
      NEW.sales_date < DATE '2014-03-01') THEN
    INSERT INTO sales_record_m1_to_m2 VALUES (NEW.*);
  ELSEIF (NEW.sales_date >= DATE '2014-03-01' AND
          NEW.sales_date < DATE '2014-05-01') THEN
    INSERT INTO sales_record_m3_to_m4 VALUES (NEW.*);
  ELSEIF (NEW.sales_date >= DATE '2014-05-01' AND
          NEW.sales_date < DATE '2014-07-01') THEN
    INSERT INTO sales_record_m5_to_m6 VALUES (NEW.*);
  ELSEIF (NEW.sales_date >= DATE '2014-07-01' AND
          NEW.sales_date < DATE '2014-09-01') THEN
    INSERT INTO sales_record_m7_to_m8 VALUES (NEW.*);
  ELSEIF (NEW.sales_date >= DATE '2014-09-01' AND
          NEW.sales_date < DATE '2014-11-01') THEN
    INSERT INTO sales_record_m9_to_m10 VALUES (NEW.*);
  ELSEIF (NEW.sales_date >= DATE '2014-11-01' AND
          NEW.sales_date < DATE '2015-01-01') THEN
    INSERT INTO sales_record_m11_to_m12 VALUES (NEW.*);
  ELSE
    RAISE EXCEPTION 'Date is out of range. Something is wrong with
    sales_record_insert_trigger() function';
  END IF;
  RETURN NULL;
END;
$$
LANGUAGE plpgsql;
```

This function will simply populate the data in the respective child table on the basis of the `sales_date` condition.

Now, the supportive trigger will call the preceding trigger function automatically whenever a user uses the INSERT, UPDATE, or DELETE operations on data in the master table.

Let's create the supportive trigger in the following manner:

```
warehouse_db=# CREATE TRIGGER sales_day_trigger
  BEFORE INSERT ON sales_record
  FOR EACH ROW
  EXECUTE PROCEDURE sales_record_insert();
```

Enabling the constraint exclusion

The final step in implementation of partitioning is enabling the constraint exclusion. Constraint exclusion is backed by the CHECK constraints that we have used in our child table's CREATE syntax. Do remember that if the constraint exclusion is disabled, then our queries will not use CHECK constraints, and as a result, every query scan will be done on all the child tables and thus will reduce performance; this is why constraint exclusion to is very important when using partitioned tables.

The steps to enable constraint exclusion are as follows:

1. Open the postgresql.conf file that is present in the data directory on your default installation path. In most cases, it is /opt/PostgreSQL/9.4/data.

2. Set constraint exclusion on with the following row in postgresql.conf:

```
constraint_exclusion = on
```

> Alternatively, you can set constraint exclusion to on using the following command on psql:
> ```
> warehouse_db=# SET constraint_exclusion = on;
> ```

Congratulations! Finally, the master table is available for the DML and DDL operations, and all the INSERT, SELECT and DELETE operations go to the child tables by date.

Performing DML operations on a partition table

Before actually performing the INSERT operations, let's first discuss the effect of the INSERT statement on the master and child tables. When a user inserts a row in the master table, our trigger sales_day_trigger will be triggered, and it will call our sales_record_insert() trigger function, and based on sales_date, the insertion will be made to a specific child table. Now, let's insert a few records into the sales_record table. We will then perform the SELECT statements to verify that records are properly populated in child tables. This can be done in the following manner:

```
warehouse_db=# INSERT INTO sales_record
   (id, sales_amount, sales_date)
VALUES
   (1, 500, TO_DATE('02/12/2014','MM/DD/YYYY'));

warehouse_db=# INSERT INTO sales_record
   (id, sales_amount, sales_date)
VALUES
```

```
    (2, 1500, TO_DATE('03/10/2014','MM/DD/YYYY'));


warehouse_db=# INSERT INTO sales_record
  (id, sales_amount, sales_date)
VALUES
    (3, 2500, TO_DATE('05/15/2014','MM/DD/YYYY'));


warehouse_db=# INSERT INTO sales_record
  (id, sales_amount, sales_date)
VALUES
    (4, 2000, TO_DATE('07/25/2014','MM/DD/YYYY'));


warehouse_db=# INSERT INTO sales_record
  (id, sales_amount, sales_date)
VALUES
    (5, 2200, TO_DATE('09/15/2014','MM/DD/YYYY'));


warehouse_db=# INSERT INTO sales_record
  (id, sales_amount, sales_date)
VALUES
    (6, 1200, TO_DATE('11/15/2014','MM/DD/YYYY'));
```

We have inserted six records, and we are now going to perform the SELECT queries on our child tables to verify that our child tables get the right data. Let's do a SELECT operation on the sales_record_m3_to_m4 table in the following manner:

```
warehouse_db=# SELECT * FROM sales_record_m3_to_m4;
 id | sales_amount | sales_date
----+--------------+------------
  2 |         1500 | 2014-03-10
(1 row)
```

Let's do a select operation on the sales_record_m9_to_m10 table in the following manner:

```
warehouse_db=# SELECT * FROM sales_record_m9_to_m10;
 id | sales_amount | sales_date
----+--------------+------------
  5 |         2200 | 2014-09-15
(1 row)
```

As you can see in the preceding result, the sales_record_m9_to_m10 child table contains the record that has sales_date for September and October.

A SELECT operation on the parent/master table will grab data from all child tables. This can be seen using the following statement:

```
warehouse_db=# SELECT * FROM sales_record;
 id | sales_amount | sales_date
----+--------------+------------
  1 |          500 | 2014-02-12
  2 |         1500 | 2014-03-10
  3 |         2500 | 2014-05-15
  4 |         2000 | 2014-07-25
  5 |         2200 | 2014-09-15
  6 |         1200 | 2014-11-15
(6 rows)
```

Handling the UPDATE and DELETE statements on a partition table

We don't need any UPDATE or DELETE triggers, the INSERT trigger is self-sufficient to handle the UPDATE or DELETE statement as well. First, let's perform an UPDATE action and verify the impact on the child table in the following manner:

```
warehouse_db=# UPDATE sales_record SET sales_date='2014-9-13'
                WHERE id = 5;
```

The preceding query will update the record of the date 2014-9-15 with id = 5.

Let's perform a SELECT operation to verify the update of the record in the following manner:

```
warehouse_db=# SELECT * FROM sales_record_m9_to_m10;
 id | sales_amount | sales_date
----+--------------+------------
  5 |         2200 | 2014-09-13
(1 row)
```

We can now verify that the record is updated and sales_date is changed to a new date, that is, 2014-09-13.

 An update on a table that can cause row movement between children requires an UPDATE trigger.

Now, let's perform a simple DELETE operation and verify the impact on partitioned tables:

```
warehouse_db=# DELETE FROM sales_record where sales_date
              = '2014-9-13';
```

Let's verify that the record is deleted from the child table using the following statement:

```
warehouse_db=# SELECT * FROM sales_record_m9_to_m10;
 id | sales_amount | sales_date
----+--------------+------------
(0 rows)
```

Since the SELECT statement did not return any record, this confirms that we have successfully deleted the record with sales_date = '2014-9-13'.

List partition

List partition is very much similar to range partition. The table is partitioned by explicitly listing which key values appear in each partition. In list partition, each partition is defined and designated based on a column value in one set of value lists, instead of one set of adjoining ranges of values. This will be done by defining each partition by means of the values IN (value_list) syntax, where value_list is a comma-separated list of values.

In the preceding sections, we have successfully created the range partition. Now for the purpose of list partition, we have to do the same task again. We will create a master table that will have a sales record along with the city information. The list partition will use the city column as a base to create the child partitions.

Let's create a master table first in the following manner:

```
warehouse_db=# CREATE TABLE sales_record_listpart
  (
  id NUMERIC primary key,
  sales_date date,
  sales_amount NUMERIC,
  city text
  );
```

Now, as we did in the preceding sections, let's create the child tables, but this time on the basis of the city list.

Create the `sales_record_list1` table in the following manner:

```
warehouse_db=# CREATE TABLE sales_record_list1
  (
  PRIMARY KEY (id, city),
  CHECK (city IN ('new york', 'sydney'))
  )
  INHERITS (sales_record_listpart);
```

Now, create the `sales_record_list2` table in the following manner:

```
warehouse_db=# CREATE TABLE sales_record_list2
  (
  PRIMARY KEY (id, city),
  CHECK (city IN ('Islamabad', 'Boston', 'London'))
  )
  INHERITS (sales_record_listpart);
```

Let's create the index for the `sales_record_list1` table:

```
warehouse_db=# CREATE INDEX list1_index ON
              sales_record_list1(city);
```

Let's create the index for the `sales_record_list2` table:

```
warehouse_db=# CREATE INDEX list2_index ON
              sales_record_list2 (city);
```

Now, create the trigger function in the following manner:

```
warehouse_db=# CREATE OR REPLACE FUNCTION
              sales_record_list_insert()
RETURNS TRIGGER AS $$
BEGIN
  IF (NEW.city IN ('new york', 'sydney')) THEN
    INSERT INTO sales_record_list1 VALUES (NEW.*);
  ELSEIF (NEW.city IN ('Islamabad', 'Boston', 'London')) THEN
    INSERT INTO sales_record_list2 VALUES (NEW.*);
  ELSE
    RAISE EXCEPTION 'CITY not present in this lists';
  END IF;
  RETURN NULL;
END;
$$
LANGUAGE plpgsql;
```

In the end, we need to create the supporting trigger in the following manner:

```
warehouse_db=# CREATE TRIGGER sales_day_trigger
  BEFORE INSERT ON sales_record_listpart
  FOR EACH ROW
  EXECUTE PROCEDURE sales_record_list_insert();
```

You can verify that the partition is linked with the master table using the following command:

```
warehouse_db=# \d+ sales_record_listpart
                    Table "sales_record_listpart"
     Column    |  Type   | Modifiers | Storage
---------------+---------+-----------+----------
 id            | numeric | not null  | main
 sales_date    | date    |           | plain
 sales_amount  | numeric |           | main
 city          | text    |           | extended
Indexes:
    "sales_record_listpart_pkey" PRIMARY KEY, btree (id)
Triggers:
    Sales_day_trigger BEFORE INSERT ON sales_record_listpart
    FOR EACH ROW EXECUTE PROCEDURE sales_record_list_insert()
Child tables: sales_record_list1,
              sales_record_list2
Has OIDs: no
```

 The preceding output is a partial output of the \d+ command

Now, let's do some quick inserts and verify that our list partition is also working how we expect it do so:

```
warehouse_db=# INSERT INTO sales_record_listpart
  (id, sales_date, sales_amount, city)
VALUES
  (1,'15-APR-2008',1200,'sydney');

warehouse_db=# INSERT INTO sales_record_listpart
  (id, sales_date, sales_amount, city)
VALUES
  (2,'15-APR-2008',1500,'Boston');

warehouse_db=# INSERT INTO sales_record_listpart
  (id, sales_date, sales_amount, city)
VALUES
```

```
    (3,'16-APR-2008',1800,'Islamabad');

warehouse_db=# INSERT INTO sales_record_listpart
    (id, sales_date, sales_amount, city)
VALUES
    (4,'20-APR-2008',1300,'new york');
```

 When you perform the preceding INSERT statements, you will observe that the INSERT query returns the INSERT 0 0 message; this is because the record is inserted in the child tables instead of the master tables.

Perform SELECT on select_record_list1 to verify that the record is inserted as expected in the following manner:

```
warehouse_db=# SELECT * FROM sales_record_list1;
 id | sales_date | sales_amount |   city
----+------------+--------------+----------
  1 | 2008-04-15 |         1200 | sydney
  4 | 2008-04-20 |         1300 | new york
(2 rows)
```

Perform SELECT on select_record_list2 to verify that the record is inserted as expected in the following manner:

```
warehouse_db=# SELECT * FROM sales_record_list2;
 id | sales_date | sales_amount |   city
----+------------+--------------+----------
  2 | 2008-04-15 |         1500 | Boston
  3 | 2008-04-16 |         1800 | Islamabad
(2 rows)
```

Summary

Let's summarize what you have learned in this chapter. You learned about partitioning a table using the parent and child table inheritance structure. You also learned about different types of partitioning that PostgreSQL supports. We also took a walk through the usage of trigger functions that handle the DML and DDL operations for a partitioned table. In the next chapter, which is about query optimization, you will learn how you can expand a database efficiently and perform database tuning.

7
Query Optimization

Query optimization is fundamental and the most important concept for a database developer to utilize the database efficiently, and this is the consequent part of database tuning. In general, query optimization is not the responsibility of the user, because after submitting the query, it's the database server optimizer's responsibility to optimize the query in the best possible way. Therefore, PostgreSQL provides ways to optimize the query. In this chapter, we will explore all these ways in detail. The important part of query optimization is studying the parameters, which involves query creation; we will discuss these parameters in detail in this chapter. We will also study query optimization by exploring the query construction and the commands that can be used to get the information of the inner working of the planner and optimizer. This is required to deduce why the query is slow and how to improve its performance; this is the main objective of this chapter. There are many ways in PostgreSQL to detect and fine-tune the query performance. This includes composing the efficient query and tuning PostgreSQL's configuration parameters.

The topics we will discuss in the following sections are:

- Query detail using EXPLAIN
- Query plan structure
- How to detect the query performance problem
- Different ways to improve the database performance

What is EXPLAIN?

The EXPLAIN command is utilized to exhibit the execution plan of the query. It shows how tables will be scanned and the estimated cost of the query. This is the first step to improve the slow query, because it will show what will happen when a query is executed. EXPLAIN has the ability to show how PostgreSQL will genuinely execute the query internally. By understanding the detail exposed by EXPLAIN, you can efficiently optimize the queries.

There are several parts to the EXPLAIN command's output, such as, scan, type, estimated start up cost, estimated query total execution time, estimated number of rows, and average width of row. Understanding all the information is the first step towards query optimization.

Let's use the EXPLAIN command on record.history as follows:

```
warehouse_db=# EXPLAIN SELECT * FROM record.history;
                          QUERY PLAN
------------------------------------------------------------------
 Seq Scan on history  (cost=0.00..1934344.66 rows=99976466 width=46)
 Planning time: 474.581 ms
(2 rows)
```

The first part of the information is the most important information in the EXPLAIN output, which is the scan type, displayed as Seq Scan in the preceding example. PostgreSQL devises the **query plan** for the query, which consists of plan nodes. The query plan is like a tree and bottom-level scans return the raw rows of the table. There are three types of scans: **sequential scans**, **index scans**, and **bitmap scans**. We will discuss the detail of each scan later in the chapter.

There are two costs involved in culling the scan: **start up cost** and **execution cost**. Both costs are estimated costs, predicated on unit of disk page fetch. In the preceding example, the start up cost is 0.00. This start up cost is the estimated start up cost of the query, which denotes the estimated time taken before output scan commences, for example, sorting time for the sort node. The estimated execution time is the total time taken to execute the query, which is 1934344.66 in our first example. The next information is the estimated number of rows, which is 99976466 in the preceding example.

For nested plans, the EXPLAIN command shows the complete list of plan and subplans. The upper plan cost is the sum of all child plans. Here is an example of the nested plan:

```
warehouse_db=# EXPLAIN SELECT COUNT(*)
   FROM record.history
   WHERE warehouse_id
```

```
    IN (SELECT warehouse_id from record.warehouse_tbl);
                          QUERY PLAN
-------------------------------------------------------------------
 Aggregate  (cost=3434597.62..3434537.63 rows=1 width=0)
   -> Hash Join  (cost=17.62..3309597.62 rows=50000000 width=0)
     Hash Cond: (history.warehouse_id = warehouse_tbl.
     warehouse_id)
     -> Seq Scan on history (cost=0.00..1934580.00 rows=100000000
     width=4)
     -> Hash  (cost=15.12..15.12 rows=200 width=4)
       -> HashAggregate  (cost=13.12..15.12 rows=200 width=4)
       Group Key: warehouse_tbl. warehouse_id
         -> Seq Scan on warehouse_tbl  (cost=0.00..12.50 rows=250
         width=4)
 Planning time: 0.241 ms
 (9 rows)
```

Working with EXPLAIN ANALYZE

EXPLAIN with the ANALYZE option shows the actual runtime of the query. This can be explained with the following example:

```
warehouse_db=# EXPLAIN ANALYZE SELECT * FROM record.history;
                          QUERY PLAN
-------------------------------------------------------------------
 Seq Scan on history (cost=0.00..1934580.00 rows=100000000
   width=46) (actual time=0.013..371995.771 rows=100000000 loops=1)
 Planning time: 0.413 ms
 Execution time: 378752.345 ms
 (3 rows)
```

In the preceding example, you can see the two rows; one is the same estimated costs, which we have already discussed, and the second row is the actual runtime. The estimated start up cost is 0.00 but actually it is not; queries require some time to start. There is more information, which is loops. Some nodes execute multiple times such as joins. In this case, loops is more than one and all costs parameters are per loop and not for whole scans.

[EXPLAIN ANALYZE can take a long time for large tables and complex queries.]

EXPLAIN VERBOSE

Now, we will dig more into EXPLAIN with EXPLAIN VERBOSE. The following is an example of EXPLAIN VERBOSE:

```
warehouse_db=# EXPLAIN VERBOSE SELECT * FROM record.history;
                              QUERY PLAN
-----------------------------------------------------------------
 Seq Scan on record.history  (cost=0.00..1934580.00 rows=100000000
   width=46)
    Output: history_id, date, amount, data, customer_id,
    warehouse_id
 Planning time: 0.093 ms
(3 rows)
```

EXPLAIN pretty formats

There is a wonderful option from where we can get a more readable output from EXPLAIN. The formatted output can be easily parsed by programs. Formatted output can be in TEXT, XML, JSON, or YAML.

Here is an example of a formatted output in JSON:

```
warehouse_db=# EXPLAIN (FORMAT JSON) SELECT * FROM record.history;
            QUERY PLAN
-----------------------------------
 [                                  +
   {                                +
     "Plan": {                      +
       "Node Type": "Seq Scan",     +
       "Relation Name": "history",  +
       "Alias": "history",          +
       "Startup Cost": 0.00,        +
       "Total Cost": 1934580.00,    +
       "Plan Rows": 100000000,      +
       "Plan Width": 46             +
     },                             +
     "Planning Time": 0.101         +
   }                                +
 ]
(2 rows)
```

Here is another formatted output in YAML:

```
warehouse_db=# EXPLAIN (FORMAT YAML) SELECT * FROM record.history;
          QUERY PLAN
---------------------------------
  - Plan:                        +
      Node Type: "Seq Scan"      +
      Relation Name: "history"   +
      Alias: "history"           +
      Startup Cost: 0.00         +
      Total Cost: 1934580.00     +
      Plan Rows: 100000000       +
      Plan Width: 46             +
    Planning Time: 0.088
  (2 rows)
```

Cost parameters

The costs in PostgreSQL are measured in arbitrary units determined by the planner's cost parameters usually measured in units of disk page fetches. The cost computation is the estimated cost loosely associated with authentic real-world numbers. The different type of cost parameters can be listed as follows:

- seq_page_cost: This is the cost to fetch sequential disk pages. By default, the cost in units of time to read is 8 K blocks, because by default, the page size is 8 K. By default, the value of this parameter is 1; hence, all other parameters have a value relative to this parameter.

- random_page_cost: This is a nonsequential read cost of disk page, that is, the time required to get the random disk page. It is a multiple of the sequential page cost (seq_page_cost). The default value is 4.

- cpu_tuple_cost: This is the cost of processing each tuple, that is, the time needed to process a single row. The default value is 0.01.

- cpu_operator_cost: This is the cost of processing each operator or function call; the default value is 0.0025.

- cpu_index_tuple_cost: This is the cost of processing each index entry during an index scan; the default value is 0.005.

The following table shows the various cost parameters along with their default values:

Parameter	Default value
seq_page_cost	1.00
random_page_cost	4.00
cpu_tuple_cost	0.01
cpu_operator_cost	0.0025
cpu_index_tuple_cost	0.005

Consider the following example for the seq_page_cost and random_page_cost parameters:

```
warehouse_db=# SELECT current_setting('seq_page_cost'),
               current_setting('random_page_cost');
 current_setting | current_setting
-----------------+-----------------
 1               | 4
(1 row)
```

 Parent nodes have the cumulative cost of all of its children.

Sequential scans

The sequential scan scans the whole table sequentially to retrieve the required rows from the table. The planner selects the sequential scan when a query is retrieving large number of rows from the table and the number of appropriate indexes found. The following is an example of a sequential scan where a query has to select all the history table's records where hist_id is greater than 1000. There is an index defined for the hist_id column but it won't help in this case:

```
warehouse_db=# EXPLAIN SELECT * FROM record.history WHERE
               history_id > 1000;
                          QUERY PLAN
--------------------------------------------------------------
 Seq Scan on history  (cost=0.00..2184580.00 rows=99998968
   width=46)
     Filter: (history_id > 1000)
 Planning time: 57.910 ms
(3 rows)
```

Any scan can be enabled or disabled using the SET command.

This SET command enables a sequential scan:

```
SET enable_seqscan = TRUE/FALSE;
```

This SET command enables an index scan:

```
SET enable_indexscan = TRUE/FALSE;
```

This SET command enables a bitmap scan:

```
SET enable_bitmapscan = TRUE/FALSE;
```

This SET command enables an index-only scan:

```
SET enable_indexonlyscan = TRUE/FALSE;
```

The next scan is automatically selected if the lower cost scan is disabled.

Index scans

An index is a way to efficiently retrieve specific rows from database. The planner chooses an index scan if any index satisfies the WHERE condition. It is faster than the normal table scan because it does not traverse the whole set of column of rows. Normally, an index is created on tables with lesser number of columns. In index scans, PostgreSQL picks only one tuple's pointer and accesses the tuple/row from the table.

An index based on all columns of table has no performance benefit.

Here is an example of an index scan:

```
warehouse_db=# EXPLAIN SELECT * FROM record.history WHERE
               history_id=1000;
                         QUERY PLAN
------------------------------------------------------------------
 Index Scan using idx on history  (cost=0.57..8.59 rows=1
 width=46)
    Index Cond: (history_id = 1000)
 Planning time: 0.142 ms
(3 rows)
```

Index-only scans

If all the columns of a query are part of the index, then the planner selects index-only scans. In this case, the tuple on the page is visible, so tuples are picked from an index instead of a heap, which is a really big performance boost. The following example shows an index-only scan:

```
warehouse_db=# EXPLAIN SELECT history_id FROM record.history WHERE
                history_id = 1000;
                            QUERY PLAN
-----------------------------------------------------------------
 Index Only Scan using idx on history  (cost=0.57..8.59 rows=1
 width=4)
    Index Cond: (history_id = 1000)
 Planning time: 0.121 ms
(3 rows)
```

In the preceding example, all the columns in the target and qual lists are part of the index; therefore, the planner selects index-only scans.

> If an index becomes inefficient or blotted, then the index must be rebuilt using the REINDEX command.

Bitmap scans

Unlike the index scan, the bitmap scan fetches all the tuple-pointers from the disks and fetches the tuple using the bitmap data structure. A bitmap scan is useful only when small numbers of rows are needed. Here is an example of a bitmap scan in which we get rows that have hist_id as 1000 or 20000:

```
warehouse_db=# EXPLAIN SELECT * FROM record.history WHERE
                history_id = 1000  AND history_id = 20000;
                            QUERY PLAN
-----------------------------------------------------------------
 Result  (cost=4.58..8.59 rows=1 width=46)
   One-Time Filter: false
     -> Bitmap Heap Scan on history  (cost=4.58..8.59 rows=1
     width=46)
       Recheck Cond: (history_id = 1000)
         -> Bitmap Index Scan on idx  (cost=0.00..4.58 rows=1
         width=0)
           Index Cond: (history_id = 1000)
 Planning time: 0.191 ms
(7 rows)
```

Common Table Expressions

To add readability and simplification to much larger and complex queries, PostgreSQL has a rich feature known as **Common Table Expressions (CTE)**. Using the WITH keyword in query, you find a way to break down the query and attain efficiency along with readability. What it does is that it can be used like an in-line view and even allows recursion to your SQL statements. Though for recursion, you have to use the WITH RECURSIVE keyword instead of simply using WITH for your queries. We will see how CTE can be used and its resultant plan node. In the following example, we will create a test_cte_scan table and using PostgreSQL's generate_series() function, we will will fabricate some data:

```
CREATE TABLE test_cte_scan
  (
  customer_id INT NOT NULL,
  order_date TIMESTAMP NOT NULL,
  filler_txt TEXT NOT NULL
  );
INSERT INTO test_cte_scan
SELECT series.id, (CURRENT_DATE - INTERVAL '500 days')::DATE
  + generate_series(1, series.id%500), repeat(' ', 10)
  FROM generate_series(1, 5000) series (id);
CREATE INDEX idx_customer_id_date ON test_cte_scan
  (customer_id, order_date DESC);
```

Now, we will demonstrate the CTE scan.

```
EXPLAIN ANALYZE WITH cte_test AS
  (SELECT EXTRACT (year FROM order_date) as year, EXTRACT (month
  FROM order_date) as month, COUNT(*) as total_customers
  FROM test_cte_scan
  GROUP BY year,month)
  SELECT year, count(*) AS tab_data
  FROM cte_test
  GROUP BY year;
                              QUERY PLAN
--------------------------------------------------------------------
 HashAggregate  (cost=37261.47..37263.47 rows=200 width=8) (actual
   time=2807.585..2807.587 rows=2 loops=1)
     CTE cte_test
       -> HashAggregate  (cost=37241.75..37249.14 rows=493
       width=8) (actual time=2807.545..2807.551 rows=17 loops=1)
         -> Seq Scan on test_cte_scan  (cost=0.00..27885.50
         rows=1247500 width=8) (actual time=0.037..1676.396
         rows=1247500 loops=1)
     -> CTE Scan on cte_test  (cost=0.00..9.86 rows=493 width=8)
     (actual time=2807.549..2807.571 rows=17 loops=1)
 Total runtime: 2807.709 ms
(6 rows)
```

Joins

By now, you have already found that for a SQL query, there can be numerous and equipollent query plans and the complexity of the query planner here is not merely culling the index scan types and estimating the cost but it is withal about joining the tables as well. Selecting the possible and optimal plan among the possible ways gets involved for each incipient table integrated into the list for each join possibility. This essentiality is going to give birth to a range of techniques available to join each table pair. We will optically discern them piecemeal and discuss how they work and differ from each other. A join takes the outer and inner tables or you can utilize left and right terms interchangeably.

Let's try expressing the relation for a join between *A* and *B*. If *A* is the outer join operand, then *B* is the inner join operand, or alternatively *A* is left and *B* is right.

Nested loop joins

A nested loop join is basically a nested FOR loop in which the relation on the right is scanned once for every row found in the relation on the left. Though this is easy to implement, it can be time consuming and useful when the finding qualifying rows operation is cheap.

 The only way to execute a **cross join** is nested loop.

The pseudocode representation of a nested loop join between *A* and *B* is as follows:

```
for each outer row in A:
  for each inner row in B:
    if join condition is true:
      output resultant row
```

In the latest PostgreSQL versions, improvement has been made to the planner's ability to use nested loops with inner index scans. Let's look at the query plan for this type of join using the `warehouse_tbl` and `history` tables:

```
warehouse_db=# EXPLAIN SELECT * FROM record.warehouse_tbl,
                record.history;
                        QUERY PLAN
--------------------------------------------------------------------
 Nested Loop  (cost=0.00..6934581.05 rows=400000000 width=291)
   -> Seq Scan on history  (cost=0.00..1934580.00 rows=100000000
   width=46)
     -> Materialize  (cost=0.00..1.06 rows=4 width=245)
```

```
    -> Seq Scan on warehouse_tbl  (cost=0.00..1.04 rows=4
    width=245)
 Planning time: 0.158 ms
 (5 rows)
```

Merge joins

A merge join or a sort-merge join works on the principle that before the join starts, each relation is first sorted on the join attributes. Scanning is performed in parallel and matching rows are thus combined. Implementation can become complex with duplicate values, so if the left one has duplicate values, then the right table can be rescanned more than once.

 Merge joins are observed when joining on the basis of equality and not on range or inequality.

Hash joins

Unlike a merge join, a hash join doesn't sort its input. Rather, it first creates a hash table from each row of the right table using its join attributes as **hash keys** and then scans the left table to find the corresponding matching rows.

It will be more evident from the query plan of the hash join on the same tables we used earlier for the nested loop join. So, let's take a look at the following hash join example:

```
warehouse_db=# EXPLAIN SELECT * FROM record.warehouse_tbl,
               record.history WHERE warehouse_tbl.warehouse_id =
               history.warehouse_id;
                         QUERY PLAN
-------------------------------------------------------------------
 Hash Join  (cost=1.09..3309581.09 rows=100000000 width=291)
   Hash Cond: (history.warehouse_id = warehouse_tbl.warehouse_id)
     -> Seq Scan on history  (cost=0.00..1934580.00 rows=100000000
     width=46)
       -> Hash  (cost=1.04..1.04 rows=4 width=245)
         -> Seq Scan on warehouse_tbl  (cost=0.00..1.04 rows=4
         width=245)
 Planning time: 0.265 ms
 (6 rows)
```

 You can create an intermediate hash table from a small table.

Hash semi and anti joins

A semi join can be exercised when the optimizer has to make sure that a key value exists on one side of the join. On the other hand, an anti join looks particularly for entries where the key value doesn't exist.

 Usually, these two types of joins are used when executing the EXISTS and NOT EXISTS expressions.

Let's use the EXISTS and NOT EXISTS expressions in our queries and then generate the plan accordingly. Generate a query using the EXISTS expression in the following statement:

```
warehouse_db=# EXPLAIN SELECT * FROM record.warehouse_tbl WHERE
               EXISTS (SELECT 1 FROM record.history where
               warehouse_tbl.warehouse_id = history.warehouse_id);
                          QUERY PLAN
----------------------------------------------------------------
 Nested Loop Semi Join  (cost=0.00..1934581.90 rows=4 width=245)
   Join Filter: (warehouse_tbl.warehouse_id = history.warehouse_id)
     -> Seq Scan on warehouse_tbl  (cost=0.00..1.04 rows=4
     width=245)
       -> Seq Scan on history  (cost=0.00..1934580.00
       rows=100000000 width=4)
 Planning time: 0.255 ms
(5 rows)
```

Generate a query using the NOT EXISTS expression in the following statement:

```
warehouse_db=# EXPLAIN SELECT * FROM record.warehouse_tbl WHERE
               NOT EXISTS (SELECT 1 FROM record.history where
               warehouse_tbl.warehouse_id = history.warehouse_id);
                          QUERY PLAN
----------------------------------------------------------------
 Nested Loop Anti Join  (cost=0.00..1934581.90 rows=1 width=245)
   Join Filter: (warehouse_tbl.warehouse_id = history.warehouse_id)
     -> Seq Scan on warehouse_tbl  (cost=0.00..1.04 rows=4
     width=245)
       -> Seq Scan on history  (cost=0.00..1934580.00
       rows=100000000 width=4)
 Planning time: 0.233 ms
(5 rows)
```

Join ordering

When the number of joins increases, so does the complexity associated in controlling it in query tuning and the optimizer. Though the query optimizer can choose plans to execute these joins in several orders with identical results, yet the most inexpensive one will be utilized. However, performing these searches for best plans can be time consuming and error prone for decisions. You can coerce the optimizer to utilize the order you consider is the optimal way to join the tables, thus reducing the orchestrating time when performing a series of explicit join operations. In this way, other plans will not be considered. This can be a subsidiary, considering if the query-construction time is huge for a complex join or when the order selected by the optimizer is worthless.

Query planning

How well you plan will decide how optimized the solution is.

To know why we need query planning is to first understand that queries are presented in a logical way of SQL statements that state to achieve a goal but queries are executed physically, and for this, even a simple-looking query at front might have to consider many constraints internally to find the most efficient way to execute a query. This, undoubtedly, is the single-line objective of the PostgreSQL query planner, that is, to determine the best way to evaluate a query.

Let's peep into what query planning has to consider before generating a plan. We will later see how this feature is exposed through EXPLAIN in detail.

Let's recall the query workflow in the following manner:

1. The SQL query is transformed into a **query tree**.
2. The query tree is tailored by the rewriter in such a way that it looks for keywords in the query tree and expands further with the provided definition.
3. The planner takes the modified parse tree as an input and generates all the feasible query paths. The planner further evaluates the path to determine the optimal path and develops a query plan for this path.
4. The query plan is modified into executable SQL queries and processed to achieve desired results.

Hence, we can summarize two basic tasks of the query planner. They are as follows:

*   List the set of plans for a given query
*   Predict the cost of executing a certain query plan

The factors the query planner has to take in consideration for an efficient plan generation (step 3 described in preceding workflow) are as follows:

- Indexes
- Access methods (sequential scan, index scan, bitmap scan, index-only scan)
- Join types (nested loop joins, hash joins, sort-merge joins)
- Sort/aggregate/pipelining

Identical results can be achieved by utilizing different accumulations of the preceding discussion, and it is evident that for a certain SQL query, there can be numerous equipollent query plans and differences associated with runtime costs, and among them, some equipollent plans can be huge.

Window functions

In *Chapter 5, Window Functions*, we discussed the detailed utilization of window functions. So, we won't be reiterating them here. As verbally expressed, "They are utilized for calculation between multiple rows, which are somehow cognate to the current query row." It can be related to the type of calculation achieved using the aggregate functions. However, in contrast to aggregate functions, a window function does not group rows into a single output row; rather, it retains their separate identities. If you are in a situation where you either have to tune your complex queries or create a custom function that has to calculate cumulative values or row numbers, you should try considering window functions as the first alternative that will not only induce maintainability but efficiency as well.

Let's take an example of the `warehouse_tbl` table again in the following manner:

```
warehouse_db=# SELECT warehouse_id, year_created, warehouse_name
            FROM warehouse_tbl;
 warehouse_id | year_created | warehouse_name
--------------+--------------+----------------
            1 |         2013 | Mark Corp
            2 |         2013 | Bill & Co
            3 |         2013 | West point
            4 |         2014 | AB Corp
            5 |         2015 | Delta Time
(5 rows)
```

Suppose we want to get the row number of the current row within its partitioning starting from 1 on the basis of the `year_created` column value. This can be done using the following statement:

```
warehouse_db=# SELECT warehouse_id, year_created, warehouse_name,
              row_number() OVER (PARTITION BY Year_created) FROM
              warehouse_tbl;
 warehouse_id | year_created | warehouse_name | row_number
--------------+--------------+----------------+------------
            1 |         2013 | Mark Corp      |          1
            2 |         2013 | Bill & Co      |          2
            3 |         2013 | West point     |          3
            4 |         2014 | AB Ccrp        |          1
            5 |         2015 | Delta Time     |          1
(5 rows)
```

Imagine that you have to maintain or build a SQL query for the preceding problem; it will not only be difficult in creating or maintaining but will also be slower if compared to the use of window functions.

Let's see the query plan for the preceding example as well:

```
                           QUERY PLAN
-----------------------------------------------------------------
 WindowAgg  (cost=21.89..26.09 rows=240 width=110) (actual
   time=6.813..11.179 rows=5 loops=1)
    -> Sort  (cost=21.89..22.49 rows=240 width=110) (actual
   time=6.806..6.807 rows=5 loops=1)
      Sort Key: w_ytd
      Sort Method: quicksort  Memory: 25kB
        -> Seq Scan on warehouse  (cost=0.00..12.40 rows=240
      width=110) (actual time=0.035..0.039 rows=5 loops=1)
 Total runtime: 11.265 ms
(6 rows)
```

Hints

PostgreSQL does not have **optimizer hints**, but there is another way to provide allusions to the optimizer. We can enable or disable features according to our requirement; if we don't want to utilize the sequential scan, then we can disable it and the planner will use the next scan for that query. We can get the benefit of hints by enabling and disabling the scans according to our need. This is an indirect way to provide hints to the planner. Let's take a look at the following index scan example:

```
warehouse_db=# EXPLAIN SELECT * FROM record.history WHERE
              history_id = 1000;
                           QUERY PLAN
```

```
-------------------------------------------------------------------
 Index Scan using idx on history  (cost=0.57..8.59 rows=1
  width=46)
    Index Cond: (history_id = 1000)
 Planning time: 0.146 ms
(3 rows)
```

In the preceding hints example, the planner culls the index scan for the query. If we don't want to utilize the index scan, then we can incapacitate the index scan using the following statement:

```
warehouse_db=# SET enable_indexscan = FALSE;
```

The result of using the preceding statement is as follows:

```
warehouse_db=# EXPLAIN SELECT * FROM record.history WHERE
               history_id = 1000;
                         QUERY PLAN
-------------------------------------------------------------------
 Bitmap Heap Scan on history  (cost=4.58..8.59 rows=1 width=46)
  Recheck Cond: (history_id = 1000)
  -> Bitmap Index Scan on idx  (cost=0.00..4.58 rows=1 width=0)
    Index Cond: (history_id = 1000)
 Planning time: 0.152 ms
(5 rows)
```

The following features can be enabled or disabled:

- enable_bitmapscan
- enable_hashjoin
- enable_indexscan
- enable_mergejoin
- enable_seqscan
- enable_tidscanenable_hashagg
- enable_indexonlyscan
- enable_material
- enable_nestloop
- enable_sort

Configuration parameters to optimize queries

Like other databases, PostgreSQL has configuration parameters that can be configured permanently or session predicated. The `postgresql.conf` file is utilized to configure most of the configuration parameters. We will only discuss the parameters that can affect the performance. They are as follows:

- `work_mem`: The disk I/O is the dominant cost factor in queries; if case queries involve a large number of complex sorts, then it can increment the disk access. If the system has lots of recollection, then the database should perform the in-recollection sorting to reduce the disk read. The `work_mem` configuration parameter is utilized to determine when the sorting will be performed in a recollection or the disk sort will be utilized. If we have lots of recollection, then the `work_mem` parameter should be set to the optimal value so that every sort can be performed in-recollection. The `work_mem` parameter is per connection for each sort; this makes it authentically hard to set the value of `work_mem`. The default value of `work_mem` is 4 MB. This can be seen using the following statement:

```
warehouse_db=# show work_mem;
 work_mem
----------
 4MB
```

The size of `work_mem` is applied to every sort performed by each connection, which makes it very hard to set the optimal value of this parameter. So, be careful while setting this parameter

The memory used by `work_mem` uses the following formula:

Memory used for by work_mem = work_mem * max_connections * (number of sort per query)

Let's consider the following example of `work_mem`:

```
warehouse_db=# EXPLAIN ANALYZE SELECT * FROM record.history
            ORDER by history_id;
                      QUERY PLAN
-----------------------------------------------------------
 Sort  (cost=24450815.88..24700815.88 rows=100000000
  width=46) (actual time=322234.459..435479.723
  rows=100000000 loops=1)
    Sort Key: history_id
    Sort Method: external sort  Disk: 5474096kB
```

```
      ->  Seq Scan on history (cost=0.00..1934580.00
      rows=100000000 width=46) (actual
      time=40.652..179067.049 rows=100000000 loops=1)
 Planning time: 0.139 ms
 Execution time: 441057.294 ms
(6 rows)
```

In the preceding example, `Sort Method` is `5474096kB`, so defining a bigger value for `work_mem` improves the performance of the sort

- `maintenance_workmem`: The memory used for maintenance work can be configured by utilizing the `maintenance_workmem` parameter. The default value is 16 MB. Increasing the value can increment the performance of the maintenance jobs such as `CREATE INDEX`, `VACUUM`, and `REINDEX`. The following statement gives the value of `maintenance_work_mem`:

```
warehouse_db=# SHOW maintenance_work_mem;
 maintenance_work_mem
----------------------
 64MB
```

- `effective_cache_size`: This parameter is used to set the estimated memory available for the operating system cache. The following statement shows the resulting value of `effective_cache_size`:

```
warehouse_db=# SHOW effective_cache_size;
 effective_cache_size
----------------------
 4GB
(1 row)
```

- `checkpoint_segments`: This parameter is used to control the checkpoint. It designates a checkpoint after the `checkpoint_segments` log file is filled, which is customarily 16 MB in size. The default value is 3. Increasing the value reduces the disk I/O, which is definitely a performance boost, and this also increases the crash recovery time. The following statement shows the default value of `checkpoint_segments`:

```
warehouse_db=# SHOW checkpoint_segments;
 checkpoint_segments
----------------------
 3
(1 row)
```

- `checkpoint_timeout`: This parameter too is used to control the checkpoints, that is, a checkpoint occurs when `checkpoint_timeout` log seconds have passed. The default value is 5 minutes. The following statement shows the default value of `checkpoint_timeout`:

```
warehouse_db=# SHOW checkpoint_timeout;
 checkpoint_timeout
--------------------
 5min
(1 row)
```

- `shared_buffers`: The `shared_buffers` parameter is used to limit the memory dedicated to caching of data in PostgreSQL. The default value is 128 MB. The following statement shows the default value of `shared_buffers`:

```
warehouse_db=# SHOW shared_buffers;
 shared_buffers
----------------
 128MB
(1 row)
```

Summary

This chapter has taken you to an advanced level, which will help you acquire the necessary database skillset to debug the queries with EXPLAIN and understand the different ways of optimizing the query using output of EXPLAIN, EXPLAIN ANALYZE and VERBOSE. Use of joins, hash, and merge joins were touched upon as well. You should be practicing the configuration parameters covered here to see performance statistics and the impact on I/O operations.

In the next chapter, we will discuss how PostgreSQL handles large objects and most importantly how to import and export them with the help of some examples.

8
Dealing with Large Objects

Databases provide data types as suitable containers to store values accordingly. You use the `int` data type to store numeric values and `char` and `varchar` data types for string values. Each data type has its own limitations with respect to the size and type of data it can store. A database solution model will be based on real life problems, therefore these are not the only types of data that you will always confront. We do not live in the ice age anymore; we have to store large-sized images, audio, video files and `varchar` is certainly not the answer to this. Objects that require huge storage size and can't be entertained with simple available data types are usually referred to as **Large Objects (LOs)** or **Binary Large OBjects (BLOBs)**. To handle these LOs, you need a LO storage mechanism that can store them easily and access them efficiently.

This chapter is all about large objects, and it is well described under this heading to give you a clear concept of LOs or BLOBs. In this chapter, we will cover the following:

- Why large objects?
- PostgreSQL large objects
- Large objects in action
- Manipulating large objects through the `libpq` client interface library

Why large objects?

We will see in a more comparative mode why and where we need large objects.

You can categorize large objects in general, based on the structure or type of data. The types you usually come across are as follows:

- Simple
- Complex

- Semi-structured
- Unstructured

Among the first two, *simple-structured* data is related to data that can be organized in simple tables and data types and *complex-structured* data is the one that deals with requirements such as that of user-defined data types.

In the age of the Internet, the types mentioned previously are not the only forms of data that you have to handle; you have XML and JSON as well. It's not interpreted by a relational database in a general way. This type of data can be categorized as *semi-structured*. Again, referring to storage of images, audio, and videos that are used massively today and can't be stored in the same way as the first three types of data because they can't be broken down into smaller logical structures for interpretation by standard means. It is hence *unstructured* data and needs a different mechanism to handle them.

PostgreSQL answers your problems with the feature of large objects that store objects of considerably huge size, and it's been there since the release of the PostgreSQL. Good things happened and over the time it's got even better.

PostgreSQL large objects

Interestingly, PostgreSQL provides two ways to store large objects with respect to each requirement you have to meet. They are as follows:

- Implementation of the BYTEA data type
- Implementation of large object storage

Though our area of interest here has been large objects, yet we will skim through some characteristics of BYTEA. It is similar to VARCHAR and text character strings, yet it has a few distinctive features as well. It can store raw or unstructured data, but character strings do not. It also allows storing of null values. VARCHAR does not permit storing zero octets, other octets, or sequences of octet values that are not valid as per database character set encoding. While using BYTEA, you can manipulate actual raw bytes, but in the case of character strings, processing is dependent on locale setting.

BYTEA when compared with large object storage comes with a big difference of storage size; each BYTEA entry permits storage of 1 GB whereas large objects allow up to 4 TB. The large object feature provides functions that help you manipulate external data in a much easier way that could be quite complex when doing the same for BYTEA.

The preceding discussion was a small comparison and analysis to show you the available choices in PostgreSQL to store binary data using BYTEA or large object storage. A requirement is the best judge to opt any of these.

Implementing large objects

Things are well remembered when they are listed and this is how we will remember PostgreSQL large objects implementation in our memory:

* Large objects, unlike BYTEA, are not a data type but an entry in a system table.

* All large objects are stored in the pg_largeobject system table.

* Each large object also has a corresponding entry in the pg_largeobject_metadata system table.

* Large objects are broken up into chunks of default size and further stored as rows in the database.

* These chunks in rows are B-tree indexed; hence, this ensures fast searches during read/write operations.

* From PostgreSQL 9.3 onwards, the maximum size of a large object in a table can be 4 TB.

* Large objects are not stored in user tables; rather, a value of the **Object Identifier (OID)** type is stored. You will use this OID value to access the large object. So, when you have to access a large object, you will reference the OID value that points to a large object present on the pg_largeobject system table.

* PostgreSQL provides the read/write **Application Program Interface (API)** that offers client- and server-side functions. Using this API, you can perform operations such as create, modify, and delete on large objects. OIDs are used in this function as a reference to access large objects, for example, to transfer the contents of any file to the database or to extract an object from the database into a file.

* From PostgreSQL 9.0 onwards, large objects now have an associated owner and a set of access permissions. Retrieving data using these functions gives you the same binary data you added. Examples of the functions are lo_create(), lo_unlink(), lo_import(), and lo_export().

* PostgreSQL provides the ALTER LARGE TABLE feature to change the definition of a large object. Remember that its only functionality is to assign a new owner.

Functions for large objects *must* be called in a *transaction block*, so when autocommit is off, make sure that you issue the BEGIN command explicitly.

Large objects in action

Now is the time to get some hands-on practice with large objects.

In this section, you will play with large objects using server functions in your SQL statements. In the following section, you will be exposed to access large objects through the libpq client interface library.

Let's search PostgreSQL for the list of functions available to access large objects:

```
postgres=# SELECT n.nspname as "Schema", p.proname as "Name",
           pg_catalog.pg_get_function_result(p.oid) as "Result
           data type", pg_catalog.pg_get_function_arguments(p.oid)
           as "Argument data types"
           FROM pg_catalog.pg_proc p LEFT JOIN
           pg_catalog.pg_namespace n ON n.oid = p.pronamespace
           WHERE p.proname ~ '^(lo_.*)$'AND
           pg_catalog.pg_function_is_visible(p.oid)
           ORDER BY 1, 2, 4;
                       List of functions
```

Schema	Name	Result data type	Argument data types
pg_catalog	lo_close	integer	integer
pg_catalog	lo_create	oid	integer
pg_catalog	lo_create	oid	oid
pg_catalog	lo_export	integer	oid, text
pg_catalog	lo_import	oid	text
pg_catalog	lo_import	oid	text, oid
pg_catalog	lo_lseek	integer	integer, integer, integer
pg_catalog	lo_lseek64	bigint	integer, bigint, integer
pg_catalog	lo_open	integer	oid, integer
pg_catalog	lo_tell	integer	integer
pg_catalog	lo_tell64	bigint	integer
pg_catalog	lo_truncate	integer	integer, integer
pg_catalog	lo_truncate64	integer	integer, bigint
pg_catalog	lo_unlink	integer	oid

```
(14 rows)
```

Suppose we need a table that can store digital pictures of huge sizes.

We will first create a table named `test_large_objects`. This can be done in the following manner:

```
postgres=# CREATE TABLE test_large_objects
  (
  picture_id INTEGER,
  name VARCHAR(30),
  picture_loc oid,
  CONSTRAINT pk_picture_id PRIMARY KEY(picture_id)
  );
```

We have an image residing in our local storage on a directory, say the `/tmp/` directory, named as `pg_disney.jpg`.

 User should have permissions to read the file.

Of course, we have not inserted a row with an image yet. Let's still query the `pg_largeobject` system table and the `test_large_objects` table for their current state. When we insert a row that includes a function call, it will affect the system table as well. Let's check the `pg_largeobject` system table using the following statement:

```
postgres=# SELECT * FROM pg_largeobject;
 loid | pageno | data
------+--------+------
(0 rows)
```

Let's check the `test_large_object` table using the following statement:

```
postgres=# SELECT * FROM test_large_objects;
 picture_id | name | picture_loc
------------+------+-------------
(0 rows)
```

Now, insert a row with the full path to the image in the following manner:

```
postgres=# INSERT INTO test_large_objects VALUES
           (1, 'pg_disney_trip', lo_import('/tmp/pg_disney.jpg'));
ERROR:  could not open server file "/tmp/pg_disney.jpg":
  Permission denied
```

 When using dummy data or images to test the large objects, make sure that they are of some size or contain data.

It was intentionally done to remind us to give appropriate permissions to the file we have to store. Giving the appropriate permission to the postgres user will let you add the file to the database. This can be done in the following manner:

```
postgres=# INSERT INTO test_large_objects VALUES
           (1, 'pg_disney_trip', lo_import('/tmp/pg_disney.jpg'));
INSERT 0 1
```

What happens here is that the lo_import() function has loaded the image inside the pg_largeobject table and returns an OID value as a reference to the large object. If you query your table, you will see the OID value and not the actual image. Let's query the user table, system table, and metadata table to see the new status.

Let's query the test_large_objects user table using the following statement:

```
postgres=# SELECT * FROM test_large_objects;
 picture_id |      name       | picture_loc
------------+-----------------+-------------
          1 | pg_disney_trip  |       74441
(1 row)
```

Now, query the pg_largeobjects system table using the following statement:

```
postgres=# SELECT loid FROM pg_largeobject;
 loid
-------
 74441
(1 row)
```

We'll now query the pg_largeobjects_metadata table using the following statement:

```
postgres=# SELECT oid FROM pg_largeobject_metadata;
  oid
-------
 74441
(1 row)
```

You will observe different OIDs when practicing these examples.

It's quite evident now that you have successfully imported an image inside a database and it has been assigned an OID as well.

You learned how to import an object; exporting or retrieving a large object can be simpler as well but with the difference that you will use the `lo_export()` function along with the OID in the following manner:

```
postgres=# SELECT lo_export(74441, '/tmp/pg_disney_second.jpg');
 lo_export
-----------
         1
(1 row)
```

 If you visit the `/tmp` directory, you will find an image with the name `pg_disney_second.jpg`.

This is how you retrieve large objects from the database, and in the end, we will try to delete this large object using the `lo_unlink()` function in the following manner:

```
postgres=# SELECT lo_unlink(74441);
 lo_unlink
-----------
         1
(1 row)
```

You might observe the usage of OID as a reference to export and unlink the large objects. To make sure that it goes well, let's query the `pg_largeobject` and `pg_largeobject_metadata` tables again.

First, query the `pg_largeobject` table using the following statement:

```
postgres=# SELECT loid FROM pg_largeobject;
 loid
--------
(0 rows)
```

Then, query the `pg_largeobject_metadata` table using the following statement:

```
postgres=# SELECT oid FROM pg_largeobject_metadata;
 oid
--------
(0 rows)
```

However, the user table still contains the row and if you try to run the `lo_unlink()` function again, it will prompt you with a meaningful message that your large object does not exist.

Use `SELECT` on the `test_large_objects` table as follows:

```
postgres=# SELECT * from test_large_objects;
 picture_id |       name      | picture_loc
------------+-----------------+-------------
          1 | pg_disney_trip  |       74441
(1 row)
```

Use the `lo_unlink()` function as follows:

```
postgres=# SELECT lo_unlink(74441);
ERROR:  large object 74441 does not exist
```

Manipulating large objects through the libpq client interface library

PostgreSQL provides multiple ways to store and access large objects. The PostgreSQL `libpq` client interface library helps you access the large objects with ease and efficiency.

This section will give you an overview of some of the main functions, their usage as per the online PostgreSQL manual, and their usage in code examples crafted for you.

For a detailed reference, you can refer to the online PostgreSQL documentation, available at `http://www.postgresql.org/docs/9.4/static/lo-interfaces.html`.

 When using these functions in client applications, include the `libpq/libpq-fs.h` header file and link with the `libpq` library.

We have designed two examples in the C programming language for you; the first example will demonstrate importing and exporting using the `libpq` library and the second will focus on accessing via the open, write, read, close, and unlink functionalities using the `libpq` client interface. Let's go through each functionality one by one:

lo_create

The syntax for the `lo_create` function is as follows:

```
Oid lo_create (PGconn *conn, int mode);
```

The `lo_create` function creates a new large object and returns an OID that is assigned to the newly created large object.

This is how we will use this in our code example (see details of the symbolic constants, that is, `INV_READ`, `INV_WRITE`, or `INV_READ | INV_WRITE` in the `libpq/libpq-fs.h` header file.):

```
lo_oid = lo_create (conn, INV_READ | INV_WRITE);
```

lo_import

We have already seen that `lo_import` is used to import a large object inside the database.

The syntax for the `lo_import` function is as follows:

```
Oid lo_import (PGconn *conn, const char *filename);
```

This function takes a filename as an argument that contains the full path of the object and returns an OID. As the file is read by the client interface library and not the server, so it must exist in the client file system with appropriate permissions.

The following example shows how `lo_import` is used:

```
lo_oid = lo_import (conn, FILE_NAME);
```

lo_export

The `lo_export` function is used to retrieve or export a large object from the system table into the operating system file.

The syntax for the `lo_export` function is as follows:

```
int lo_export (PGconn *conn, Oid lobjId, const char *filename);
```

The following example shows how `lo_export` is used:

```
lo_export (conn, lo_oid, FILE_NAME)
```

You will now be shown the first part of the code examples we were referring to. In the imp_exp.c example, we first connected to the PostgreSQL database; after a successful connection, we imported the imp.jpg file into the database using lo_import, and then we exported it as exp.jpg from the database using the OID returned in lo_export. How to connect and play with the PostgreSQL database through libpq is explained in detail later in the chapter. So for now, you need not be worried of how things are working here. As said earlier, to grasp it firmly, revisit the code examples after reading the next chapter.

The first part of the code example is as follows:

```c
/*-------------------------------------------------------------------
 *
 *imp_exp.c
 *Accessing large objects using lo_export and lo_import
 *
 *IDENTIFICATION
 *imp_exp.c
 *
 *-------------------------------------------------------------------
 */
#include <stdio.h>
#include <sys/types.h>
#include <stdlib.h>
#include <limits.h>
#include "libpq-fe.h"
#include "libpq/libpq-fs.h"
#define FILE_TO_EXPORT    "exp.jpg"
#define FILE_TO_IMPORT    "imp.jpg"

int main(int argc, char **argv)
{
  PGconn *conn;
  PGresult *res;
  int lo_oid;

/* Connect to Database testdb */
  conn = PQsetdb(NULL, NULL, NULL, NULL, "testdb");
  if (PQstatus(conn) == CONNECTION_BAD)
  {
    fprintf(stderr, "connection to database failed\n");
    fprintf(stderr, "%s", PQerrorMessage(conn));
    return -1;
  }
```

```
/* Execute the command BEGIN */
  res = PQexec(conn, "BEGIN");
  PQclear(res);

/* Import file to the database */
  lo_oid = lo_import(conn, FILE_TO_IMPORT);
  if (lo_oid < 0)
  {
    fprintf(stderr, "%s\n", PQerrorMessage(conn));
    PQfinish(conn);
    return -1;
  }
  res = PQexec(conn, "END");
  PQclear(res);

  res = PQexec(conn, "BEGIN");
  PQclear(res);

  if (lo_export(conn, lo_oid, FILE_TO_EXPORT) < 0)
  {
    fprintf(stderr, "%s\n", PQerrorMessage(conn));
    PQfinish(conn);
    return -1;
  }
  res = PQexec(conn, "END");
  PQclear(res);

  PQfinish(conn);
  fprintf(stdout, "file '%s' successful imported using 'lo_import'
  and then exported to '%s' using 'imp_export'\n", FILE_TO_IMPORT,
  FILE_TO_EXPORT);
  return lo_oid;
}
```

lo_open

The lo_open function is used to open a large object for reading or writing.

The syntax for the lo_open function is as follows:

```
int lo_open(PGconn *conn, Oid lobjId, int mode);
```

The `lo_open` function returns a large object descriptor to be used in `lo_read`, `lo_write`, `lo_lseek`, `lo_lseek64`, `lo_tell`, `lo_tell64`, `lo_truncate`, `lo_truncate64`, and `lo_close`.

The following example shows how `lo_open` is used:

```
lo_fd = lo_open(conn, lo_oid, INV_READ);
```

lo_write

The syntax for the `lo_write` function is as follows:

```
int lo_write(PGconn *conn, int fd, const char *buf, size_t len);
```

This function writes `len` bytes from `buf` (which must be at least of the size `len`) to the large object descriptor `fd`. The number of bytes actually written is returned and always equal to `len` unless there is an error where the return value is `i1-1`.

The following example shows how `lo_write` is used:

```
r = lo_write(conn, lo_fd, buf, n);
```

lo_read

The syntax for the `lo_read` function is as follows:

```
int lo_read(PGconn *conn, int fd, char *buf, size_t len);
```

Explanation is almost the same as `lo_write` with the difference of operation; here, it reads up to `len` bytes from the large object descriptor `fd` into `buf` of the size `len`. The `fd` argument should be returned by the previously mentioned `lo_open` function. The number of bytes actually read is returned, and it will be less than `len` if the end of the large object is reached first. In the case of an error, the return value is `-1`.

The following example shows how `lo_read` is used:

```
n = lo_read(conn, lo_fd, buf, 512);
```

Though similar in behavior to `lo_lseek`, `lo_read` can accept an offset larger than 2 GB and can deliver a result larger than 2 GB.

lo_close

You can close a large object descriptor by calling `lo_close`.

The syntax for the `lo_close` function is as follows:

```
int lo_close(PGconn *conn, int fd);
```

Here `fd` is a large object descriptor returned by `lo_open`. On success, `lo_close` returns `0`.

The following example shows how `lo_close` is used:

```
lo_close(conn, lo_fd);
```

In case of an error, the return value is `-1`.

lo_unlink

To remove a large object from the database, call the `lo_unlink` function.

The syntax for the `lo_unlink` function is as follows:

```
int lo_unlink(PGconn *conn, Oid lobjId);
```

The `lobjId` argument specifies the OID of the large object to remove. It will return `1` if it is successful and `-1` if failed.

Now we jump to the second example we mentioned previously. In this example, a different approach is used to access large objects. Instead of import and export functions, we used the `lo_write` and `lo_read` functions to achieve the same.

The PostgreSQL manual states the following:

> *"Any large object descriptors that remain open at the end of a transaction will be closed automatically."*

The second example is as follows:

```
/*-------------------------------------------------------------
 *
 *read_write.c
 *Accessing large objects using lo_read and lo_write
 *
 *IDENTIFICATION
 *imp_exp.c
 *-------------------------------------------------------------
 */
#include <stdio.h>
#include <sys/types.h>
#include <stdlib.h>
#include <limits.h>
#include <fcntl.h>
#include <unistd.h>
```

```c
#include "libpq-fe.h"
#include "libpq/libpq-fs.h"
#define FILE_TO_EXPORT    "exp.jpg"
#define FILE_TO_IMPORT    "imp.jpg"

int main(int argc, char **argv)
{
  PGconn *conn;
  PGresult *res;
  int lo_oid;
  int fd, lo_fd;
  int n;
  char buf[1024];
  int r;

  /* Connect to Database testdb */
  conn = PQsetdb(NULL, NULL, NULL, NULL, "testdb");
  if (PQstatus(conn) == CONNECTION_BAD)
  {
    fprintf(stderr, "connection to database failed\n");
    fprintf(stderr, "%s", PQerrorMessage(conn));
    return -1;
  }

  /* Execute the command BEGIN */
  res = PQexec(conn, "BEGIN");
  PQclear(res);

  fd = open(FILE_TO_IMPORT, O_RDONLY, 0666);
  if (fd < 0)
  {
    fprintf(stderr, "open: failed to open file %s\n",
    FILE_TO_IMPORT);
    fprintf(stderr, "%s", PQerrorMessage(conn));
    return 0;
  }

  lo_oid = lo_creat(conn, INV_READ | INV_WRITE);
  if (lo_oid < 0)
  {
    fprintf(stderr, "lo_create: failed to create object\n");
    fprintf(stderr, "%s", PQerrorMessage(conn));
    return 0;
  }
```

```
lo_fd = lo_open(conn, lo_oid, INV_WRITE);
for(;;)
{
  n = read(fd, buf, 1024);
  if (n <= 0)
    break;
  r = lo_write(conn, lo_fd, buf, n);
  if (r < n)
    fprintf(stderr, "write: failed to write object\n");
}
lo_close(conn, lo_fd);
close(fd);

res = PQexec(conn, "END");
PQclear(res);

res = PQexec(conn, "BEGIN");
PQclear(res);

fd = open(FILE_TO_EXPORT, O_CREATE | O_WRONLY, 0666);
if (fd < 0)
{
  fprintf(stderr, "open: failed to open file %s\n",
  FILE_TO_EXPORT);
  return 0;
}

lo_fd = lo_open(conn, lo_oid, INV_READ);
if (lo_fd < 0)
{
  fprintf(stderr, "lo_open: failed to create object\n");
  fprintf(stderr, "%s", PQerrorMessage(conn));
  return 0;
}

fd = open(FILE_TO_EXPORT, O_CREATE | O_WRONLY, 0666);
if (fd < 0)
{
  fprintf(stderr, "open: failed to open file %s\n",
  FILE_TO_EXPORT);
  return 0;
}
```

```
for (;;)
{
  n = lo_read(conn, lo_fd, buf, 1024);
  if (n <= 0)
    break;

  r = write(fd, buf, n);
  if (r < n)
  {
    fprintf(stderr, "write: failed to write object\n");
    break;
  }
}

lo_close(conn, lo_fd);
close(fd);

res = PQexec(conn, "END");
PQclear(res);
PQfinish(conn);

fprintf(stdout, "file '%s' successfully imported using
'lo_write' and then exported to '%s' using 'lo_read'\n",
FILE_TO_IMPORT, FILE_TO_EXPORT);
return lo_oid;
}
```

 Usage of both approaches is clear from the fact that you can use import/export when you have to access the complete file/binary data *but* read/write allows processing on selective parts of the binary data stored as a large object.

For readers, here are the steps to build the code and content of the make file for a quick reference.

Use the make command to build the code in the following manner:

```
make imp_exp
make read_write
make clean
```

The following is the content of `Makefile`:

```
CC=gcc
POSTGRESQL_INCLUDE=/usr/local/pgsql.master/include
POSTGRESQL_LIB=/usr/local/pgsql.master/lib
CFLAGS=-I$(POSTGRESQL_INCLUDE)
LD_FLAGS=-L$(POSTGRESQL_LIB)

imp_exp:
    $(CC) imp_exp.c -o imp_exp $(CFLAGS) $(LD_FLAGS) -lpq
read_write:
    $(CC) read_write.c -o read_write $(CFLAGS) $(LD_FLAGS) -
    lpq
clean:
    rm -rf *.o imp_exp read_write
```

Summary

This chapter has tried to build your clear concepts about PostgreSQL large objects, their usage, and implementation. You not only learned why and when to use large objects, but got hands-on practice on how to use them as well. Accessing them through libpq (C-based) client interface library has widened your scope for large object access and strengths of libpq. In fact, a whole chapter is designed to explain libpq in much detail, and the good news is, this is the next chapter!

9
Communicating with PostgreSQL Using LibPQ

The libpq library is a PostgreSQL client library to communicate with the PostgreSQL server. The purpose of this chapter is to write the C program to connect to the PostgreSQL server and execute queries in the C programming language. In this chapter, we will explore communication with PostgreSQL using libpq, which includes learning about all the library functions and their utilization with sufficient C code examples. We will also discuss the blocking and nonblocking behavior of libpq functions.

Connecting and disconnecting to PostgreSQL

The libpq library provides multiple functions and mechanisms to connect to the PostgreSQL server. We will discuss each and every function that is involved in establishing a connection to the backend. An application can have multiple connections with the PostgreSQL database, but needs to maintain the PGconn pointer for each and every connection. The PGconn pointer is a connection object and a function used to establish a connection. It returns the pointer that the application needs to store and use for subsequent functions to query the database. This object must be closed when the connection to the server is no longer needed because the code must release resources that the PostgreSQL runtime allocates.

Using PQconnectdb

The PQconnectdb function is the most basic function to connect to the PostgreSQL backend. This function takes only one parameter: the conninfo string. The syntax for PQconnectdb is as follows:

```
PGconn *PQconnectdb (const char *conninfo);
```

The conninfo string is a space-delimited string that contains the keyword value pairs, for example, keyword = 'foo'. Here is the list of all conninfo keywords:

- hostaddr: This is the IP address of the PostgreSQL server
- host: This is the hostname of the PostgreSQL server; it can be the name of the path of the Unix domain socket. The default value is the /tmp directory

 If the operating system does not support Unix domain sockets, the default value is localhost.

- port: This is the port number of the PostgreSQL server; the default port is 5432
- dbname: This is the name of the database we need to connect to; the default value for this is the username
- user: This is the username to connect as; the default is the operating system user
- password: This is the password used during authentication
- connect_timeout: The connect_timeout keyword shows how long the PQconnectdb function waits before giving up

Here are some more options that are not commonly used:

- client_encoding
- options
- application_name
- fallback_application_name
- keepalives
- keepalives_idle
- keepalives_interval
- keepalives_count
- tty

- sslmode
- disable
- allow
- verify-ca
- verify-full
- requiressl
- sslcert
- sslkey
- sslrootcert
- sslcrl
- requirepeer
- krbsrvname
- gsslib
- service

The details of these values can be found at http://www.postgresql.org/docs/9.4/static/libpq-connect.html#LIBPQ-PARAMKEYWORDS.

 If you see the following kind of error, then it is due to an error in the conninfo string:

```
missing "=" after "port" in connection info string
```

Using PQconnectdbParams

The PQconnectdbParams function is a variant of the PQconnectdb function. Like PQconnectdb, this function takes a two-dimension array of keys and values instead of a single key-value pair string. This function only differs in the function argument to PQconnectdb. The syntax for PQconnectdbParams is as follows:

```
PGconn *PQconnectdbParams(const char **keywords,
                          const char **values,
                          int expand_dbname);
```

Using PQsetdbLogin

The PQsetdbLogin function is another variant to connect to the PostgreSQL server. This function has a limited number of parameters and all other parameters previously discussed are used as default values. The syntax for PQsetdbLogin is as follows:

```
PGconn *PQsetdbLogin (const char *pghost,
                      const char *pgport,
                      const char *pgoptions,
                      const char *pgtty,
                      const char *dbName,
                      const char *login,
                      const char *pwd);
```

> Whenever you get the following error message while connecting to PostgreSQL, it means that the PostgreSQL server is not running, at least not on the 5432 port:
>
> ```
> connection to database failed
> could not connect to server: No such file or directory
> Is the server running locally and accepting connections
>     on Unix domain socket "/tmp/.s.PGSQL.5432"?
> ```
>
> You need to check the host and port on which the PostgreSQL server is running.

Using PQsetdb

The PQsetdb function is not a function but is macro defined, which calls the PQsetdbLogin function with the default username and password. The syntax for PQsetdb is as follows:

```
PGconn *PQsetdb(char *pghost,
               char *pgport,
               char *pgoptions,
               char *pgtty,
               char *dbName);
```

Here is the complete example of establishing a connection using all the methods previously discussed:

```
/*--------------------------------------------------------------
 *
 *connection.c
 *Connecting PostgreSQL Server using libpq
 *
 *IDENTIFICATION
 *connection.c
 *
 *--------------------------------------------------------------
 */
#include<stdio.h>
#include<sys/types.h>
#include<stdlib.h>
#include<limits.h>
#include "libpq-fe.h"
#include "libpq/libpq-fs.h"
charconninfo[] = "hostaddr = '127.0.0.1' port = '5432' dbname =
                  'testdb'";
char *keyword[] = {"hostaddr", "port", "dbname"};
char *value[] = {"127.0.0.1", "5432", "testdb"};
int main(int argc, char **argv)
{
  PGconn *conn;    /* Connection Object */
  /* Connect database using PQsetdb */
  conn = PQsetdb(NULL, NULL, NULL, NULL, "testdb");
  if (PQstatus(conn) == CONNECTION_BAD)
  {
    fprintf(stderr, "connection to database failed using
    PQsetdb");
    fprintf(stderr, "%s", PQerrorMessage(conn));
    return -1;
  }
  fprintf(stdout, "Connection to database established using
  PQsetdb\n");
  PQfinish(conn);

  /* Connect database using PQconnectdb */
  conn = PQconnectdb(conninfo);
  if (PQstatus(conn) == CONNECTION_BAD)
  {
    fprintf(stderr, "connection to database failed using
    PQconnectdb\n");
```

```
      fprintf(stderr, "%s", PQerrorMessage(conn));
      return -1;
  }
  fprintf(stdout, "Connection to database established using
  PQconnectdb\n");
  PQfinish(conn);

  /* Connect database using PQconnectdbParams */
  conn = PQconnectdbParams((const char **)keyword, (const char
  **)value, 1);
  if (PQstatus(conn) == CONNECTION_BAD)
  {
    fprintf(stderr, "connection to database failed using
    PQconnectdbParams\n");
    fprintf(stderr, "%s", PQerrorMessage(conn));
    return -1;
  }
  fprintf(stdout, "Connection to database established using
  PQconnectdbParams\n");
  PQfinish(conn);

  /* Connect database using PQsetdbLogin */
  conn = PQsetdbLogin("127.0.0.1", "5432", NULL, NULL, "testdb",
                      "foo", "bar");
  if (PQstatus(conn) == CONNECTION_BAD)
  {
    fprintf(stderr, "connection to database failed using
    PQsetdbLogin\n");
    fprintf(stderr, "%s", PQerrorMessage(conn));
    return -1;
  }
  fprintf(stdout, "Connection to database established using
  PQsetdbLogin\n");
  PQfinish(conn);

  return 0;
}
```

The following is the content of `MakeFile` to compile all the examples:

```
CC=gcc
POSTGRESQL_INCLUDE=/usr/local/pgsql.master/include
POSTGRESQL_LIB=/usr/local/pgsql.master/lib
CFLAGS=-I$(POSTGRESQL_INCLUDE)
LD_FLAGS=-L$(POSTGRESQL_LIB)

all:
    $(CC) connection.c -o connection $(CFLAGS) $(LD_FLAGS) -
    lpq
    $(CC) exec.c -o exec $(CFLAGS) $(LD_FLAGS) -lpq
    $(CC) retrieve.c -o retrieve $(CFLAGS) $(LD_FLAGS) -lpq
connection:
    $(CC) connection.c -o connection $(CFLAGS) $(LD_FLAGS) -
    lpq
exec:
    $(CC) exec.c -o exec $(CFLAGS) $(LD_FLAGS) -lpq
retrieve:
    $(CC) retrieve.c -o retrieve $(CFLAGS) $(LD_FLAGS) -lpq
clean:
    rm -rf *.o connection exec retrieve
```

Using PQfinish

The PQfinish function is used to close the connection with the server. It takes the connection object PGconn pointer returned by the PQconnectdb, PQsetdbLogin, or PQsetdb function. The syntax for PQfinish is as follows:

```
Void PQfinish(PGconn *conn);
```

Using PQreset

The PQreset function closes the previous connection and establishes a new connection. Sometimes, we need a new connection after closing the previous connection. Instead of calling PQfinish and PQconnectdb, the PQreset function closes the connection and reconnects with the server. The syntax for PQreset is as follows:

```
Void PQreset(PGconn *conn);
```

Establishing a connection asynchronously

The libpq library provides functions to connect to the PostgreSQL database asynchronously; these functions are called nonblocking functions. The nonblocking functions do not block and return immediately. The libpq library has functions that are both variant blocking and nonblocking connection functions. We've already discussed the blocking functions, and now it's time to discuss nonblocking functions.

Using PQconnectStartParams

The PQconnectStartParams function is a nonblocking variant of the PQconnectdbParams function. The complete connection is made in an application loop rather than inside the library function. The syntax for PQconnectStartParams is as follows:

```
PGconn *PQconnectStartParams(const char **keywords,
                             const char **values,
                             int expand_dbname);
```

Using PQconnectStart

The PQconnectStart function is a nonblocking variant of the PQconnectdb function. Like the PQconnectStartParams function, it also does not block. The syntax for PQconnectdbParams is as follows:

```
PGconn *PQconnectStart(const char *conninfo);
```

Using PQconnectPoll

The PQconnectPoll function is used to poll the connection status of a connection. The syntax for PQconnectPoll is as follows:

```
PostgresPollingStatusType PQconnectPoll(PGconn *conn);
```

The function can return the following values:

Functions	Value
PGRES_POLLING_FAILED	0
PGRES_POLLING_READING	1
PGRES_POLLING_WRITING	2
PGRES_POLLING_OK	3
PGRES_POLLING_ACTIVE	4

Using PQresetStart

The PQresetStart function is a nonblock variant of PQreset. Like other nonblocking functions, it will not block and the whole connection is established in an application loop, which means that the user needs to pool the status under connect, reset, or not connected. The syntax for PQresetStart is as follows:

```
Int PQresetStart(PGconn *conn);
```

Using PQresetPoll

The PQresetPoll function is used to poll the reset status. The syntax for PQresetPoll is as follows:

```
PostgresPollingStatusType PQresetPoll(PGconn *conn);
```

Connection-supporting functions

Alongside core library function, the libpq library provides some utility functions. Here are some of the utility functions.

Using PQconninfoParse

The PQconninfoParse function parses the string and returns the PQconninfoOption pointer. The syntax for PQconninfoParse is as follows:

```
PQconninfoOption *PQconninfoParse(const char *conninfo,
                                  char **errmsg);
```

Using PQpingParams

The `PQpingParams` function returns the server status. The syntax for `PQpingParams` is as follows:

```
PGPing PQpingParams(const char **keywords,
                    const char **values,
                    int expand_dbname);
```

The `PQpingParams` function can return the following values:

- `PQPING_OK`: This means that the server is available, that is, the server is accepting connections
- `PQPING_REJECT`: This means that the server is rejecting the connections
- `PQPING_NO_RESPONSE`: This means that there is no response from the server
- `PQPING_NO_ATTEMPT`: This means that there is a bad parameter and no connection attempt was made

Executing a query

We have discussed how to connect to the PostgreSQL server; the second step is executing the query. The `libpq` library also provides multiple functions to execute the query in a similar way to how it provides multiple functions to connect to the PostgreSQL server.

Using PQexec

The `PQexec` function sends the command (query) to the connected PostgreSQL server. The first parameter is the same connection object returned by the connection functions discussed previously. The syntax for `PQexec` is as follows:

```
PGresult *PQexec(PGconn *conn, const char *command);
```

Using PQexecParams

In the `PQexec` function, there is only one parameter other than the `PGconn` object that is a command string. So, if we want to send the command where some values are outside the command string, then we need the `PQexecParams` function. The syntax for `PQexecParams` is as follows:

```
PGresult *PQexecParams(PGconn *conn,
                       const char *command,
                       int nParams,
                       const Oid *paramTypes,
                       const char * const *paramValues,
                       const int *paramLengths,
                       const int *paramFormats,
                       insert resultFormat);
```

This function takes extra arguments that can be used to supply the extra parameter outside the command. They are as follows:

- `nParams`: This shows the total number of parameters
- `paramTypes`: This shows the type of parameters
- `paramValue`: This shows the parameter's value array
- `paramLengths`: This shows the length of the parameter array
- `paramFormats`: This shows that the parameters are binary (1) or text (0)

Executing prepared statements

PostgreSQL supports prepared statements. A prepared statement is used to efficiently execute the same or similar query repeatedly. First, the query is prepared in the form of a template using **placeholder** and values are substituted during execution. In PostgreSQL, the `$` sign is used to identify the placeholder.

Using PQprepare

The `PQprepare` function submits a request to create a prepared statement with the given parameters and waits for completion. The syntax for `PQprepare` is as follows:

```
PGresult *PQprepare(PGconn *conn,
                    const char *stmtName,
                    const char *query,
                    int nParams,
                    const Oid *paramTypes);
```

The PQprepare function is supported only in the protocol version 3.0 and higher. In the case of a version less than 3.0, this function will fail.

The parameters for the PQprepare function are as follows:

- stmtName: This is the name of the prepared statement
- query: This is the query string
- nParams: This is the number of parameters
- paramTypes: This shows the data types of parameters

An unnamed portal will be created if stmtName is an empty string and the previous unnamed portal will be overwritten.

Using PQexecPrepared

After preparing the query using PQprepare, we can execute the query using PQexecPrepared. The PQexecPrepared function executes the previously prepared statement. Its syntax is as follows:

```
PGresult *PQexecPrepared(PGconn *conn,
                         const char *stmtName,
                         int nParams,
                         const char * const *paramValues,
                         const int *paramLengths,
                         const int *paramFormats,
                         int resultFormat);
```

The parameters for the PQexecPrepared function are as follows:

- paramValues: This shows the values of the array of parameters
- paramLengths: This shows the length of the array of parameters
- paramFormats: This shows the format of the array of parameters
- resultFormat: This shows the result in the text or binary format

The PQexecPrepared function executes the query, which was prepared using the PQprepare function. This function uses stmtName to identify which query needs to be executed.

Prepared queries are parsed and planned only once, but nonprepared queries are parsed and planned every time.

Here is a complete example of how to establish a connection and execute a query using the connection and execution functions discussed:

```c
/*-------------------------------------------------------------------
 *
 *exec.c
 *Executing queries using libpq
 *
 *IDENTIFICATION
 *exec.c
 *
 *-------------------------------------------------------------------
 */
#include <stdio.h>
#include <sys/types.h>
#include <stdlib.h>
#include <limits.h>
#include "libpq-fe.h"
#include "libpq/libpq-fs.h"
char conninfo[] = "hostaddr = '127.0.0.1' port = '5432' dbname =
                   'testdb'";
Oid paramTypes[] = {23, 25};
int paramLengths[] = {-1, 5};
int paramFormats[] = {0, 0};

int main(int argc, char **argv)
{
  PGconn *conn; /* Connection Object */
  PGresult *result;
  char *paramValues[] = {"2", "bar-2"};

  conn = PQconnectdb(conninfo);
  if (PQstatus(conn) == CONNECTION_BAD)
  {
    fprintf(stderr, "connection to database failed\n");
    fprintf(stderr, "%s", PQerrorMessage(conn));
    return -1;
  }

  /* Execute a query using PQexec */
  result = PQexec(conn, "CREATE TABLE foo (id INTEGER, name
  TEXT)");
```

```c
if (result == NULL || PQresultStatus(result) !=
PGRES_COMMAND_OK)
{
  fprintf(stderr, "failed to execute query using PQexec\n");
  fprintf(stderr, "%s", PQerrorMessage(conn));
  return -1;
}

result = PQexec(conn, "INSERT INTO foo VALUES(1, 'bar-1')");
if (result == NULL || PQresultStatus(result) !=
PGRES_COMMAND_OK)
{
  fprintf(stderr, "failed to execute query using PQexec\n");
  fprintf(stderr, "%s", PQerrorMessage(conn));
  return -1;
}

/* Execute a query using PQexecParams */
result = PQexecParams(conn, "INSERT INTO foo VALUES($1, $2)",
                      2, paramTypes, (const char *
                      const*)paramValues, paramLengths,
                      paramFormats, 0);
if (result == NULL || PQresultStatus(result) !=
PGRES_COMMAND_OK)
{
  fprintf(stderr, "failed to execute query using
  PQexecParams\n");
  fprintf(stderr, "%s", PQerrorMessage(conn));
  return -1;
}

/* Execute a prepared query */
result = PQprepare(conn, "test", "INSERT INTO foo VALUES($1,
                   $2)", 2, paramTypes);

paramValues[0] = "3";
paramValues[1] = "bar-3";
result = PQexecPrepared(conn, "test", 2, (const char *
                        const*)paramValues, paramLengths,
                        paramFormats, 0);
if (result == NULL || PQresultStatus(result) !=
PGRES_COMMAND_OK)
{
```

```
        fprintf(stderr, "failed to execute query using
        PQexecPrepared\n");
        fprintf(stderr, "%s", PQerrorMessage(conn));
        return -1;
    }

    PQfinish(conn);
    return 0;
}
```

Retrieving data

Now, the next step is to get data from PostgreSQL. Here are the functions that are used to extract data after query execution.

Using PQntuples

The PQntuples function returns the number of rows normally called tuples in the result. Its syntax is as follows:

```
int PQntuples(const PGresult *res);
```

 A value larger than 32 bits might overflow.

Using PQnfields

The PQnfields function returns the number of columns in each row. The syntax for PQnfields is as follows:

```
int PQnfields(const PGresult *res);
```

Using PQfname

The PQfname function returns the name of the column associated with the column_number argument. The syntax for PQfname is as follows:

```
char *PQfname(const PGresult *res,
              int column_number);
```

Using PQfnumber

The `PQfnumber` function returns the column number associated with the `column_name` argument. The syntax for `PQfnumber` is as follows:

```
int PQfnumber(const PGresult *res,
              const char *column_name);
```

The following is a code snippet to explain the `PQfnumber` function:

```
ntuples = PQntuples(result);
for (i = 0; i < ntuples; i++)
{
  char *id, *name;
  /* Get the column number of column "id" and "name" */
  int id_col = PQfnumber(result, "id");
  int name_col = PQfnumber(result, "name");
  id = PQgetvalue(result, i, id_col);
  name = PQgetvalue(result, i, name_col);
  fprintf ("Data: id = %s, name = %s\n", id, name);
}
```

Using PQftable

In complex queries where multiple tables are referenced, we need to know the table OID from which that column is fetched. The `PQftable` function gets the OID of table of that particular column in the result set.

The syntax for `PQftable` is as follows:

```
Oid PQftable(const PGresult *res,
             int column_number);
```

The following is a code snippet to explain the `PQftable` function:

```
ntuples = PQntuples(result);
for (i = 0; i < ntuples; i++)
{
  char *id, *name;
  int id_col = PQfnumber(result, "id");
  int name_col = PQfnumber(result, "name");
  /* Get Table oid of column "id" */
  int oid = PQftable(result, id_col);
  fprintf(stdout, "Table oid is = %d \n", oid);
}
```

Using PQftablecol

The PQftablecol function returns the column number within a table. The syntax for PQftablecol is as follows:

```
int PQftablecol(const PGresult *res,
                int column_number);
```

Using PQfformat

The PQfformat function returns the format of a column. The syntax for PQfformat is as follows:

```
int PQfformat(const PGresult *res,
              int column_number);
```

Using PQftype

The PQftype function returns the type of a column. The syntax for PQftype is as follows:

```
Oid PQftype(const PGresult *res, int column_number);
```

Using PQfmod

The PQfmod function returns the type modifier of a column. The syntax for PQfmod is as follows:

```
int PQfmod(const PGresult *res,
           int column_number);
```

Using PQfsize

The PQfsize function returns the size of the column. The syntax for PQfsize is as follows:

```
int PQfsize(const PGresult *res,
            int column_number);
```

Using PQbinaryTuples

The PQbinaryTuples function returns whether the result is binary or text (1 for binary and 0 for text). The syntax for PQbinaryTuples is as follows:

```
int PQbinaryTuples(const PGresult *res);
```

Using PQgetvalue

The PQgetvalue function returns the value of the column of a single row. The syntax for PQgetvalue is as follows:

```
char *PQgetvalue(const PGresult *res,
                 int row_number,
                 int column_number);
```

Using PQgetisnull

The PQgetisnull function is used to check whether the value of the column of a particular row is null. If the value is null there is no need to get the value from the table. The syntax for PQgetisnull is as follows:

```
int PQgetisnull(const PGresult *res,
                int row_number,
                int column_number);
```

The following is a code snippet to explain the PQgetisnull function:

```
ntuples = PQntuples(result);
for (i = 0; i < ntuples; i++)
{
  char *id, *name;
  int id_col = PQfnumber(result, "id");
  int name_col = PQfnumber(result, "name");
  int oid = PQftable(result, id_col);
  fprintf(stdout, "id is %s \n", PQgetisnull(result, i, id_col)?
  "NULL": "NOT NULL");
  fprintf(stdout, "name is %s \n", PQgetisnull(result, i,
  name_col)? "NULL": "NOT NULL");
}
```

Using PQgetlength

The PQgetlength function returns the actual length of the column of a particular row. The syntax for PQgetlength is as follows:

```
int PQgetlength(const PGresult *res,
                int row_number,
                int column_number);
```

Using PQnparams

The PQnparams function returns the total number of parameters of a prepared statement. The syntax for PQnparams is as follows:

```
int PQnparams(const PGresult *res);
```

Using PQparamtype

The PQparamtype function returns the data type of the indicated statement parameter. The syntax for PQparamtype is as follows:

```
Oid PQparamtype(const PGresult *res, int param_number);
```

Here is the example to select the data from the PostgreSQL server. The following program shows the usage of the PQexec, PQntuples, PQfnumber, and PQfinish functions:

```
/*-------------------------------------------------------------------
 *
 *retrieve.c
 *Retrieving data using libpq
 *
 *IDENTIFICATION
 *retrieve.c
 *
 *-------------------------------------------------------------------
 */
#include <stdio.h>
#include <sys/types.h>
#include <stdlib.h>
#include <limits.h>
#include "libpq-fe.h"
#include "libpq/libpq-fs.h"

char conninfo[] = "hostaddr = '127.0.0.1' port = '5432' dbname =
  'postgres'";

int main(int argc, char **argv)
{
  PGconn *conn; /* Connection Object */
  PGresult *result;
  int ntuples;
  int i;
```

```c
  conn = PQconnectdb(conninfo);
  if (PQstatus(conn) == CONNECTION_BAD)
  {
    fprintf(stderr, "connection to database failed\n");
    fprintf(stderr, "%s", PQerrorMessage(conn));
    return -1;
  }

  /* Execute a query using PQexec */
  result = PQexec(conn, "SELECT id, name FROM foo LIMIT 3");
  if (result == NULL || PQresultStatus(result) != PGRES_TUPLES_OK)
  {
    fprintf(stderr, "failed to execute query using PQexec\n");
    fprintf(stderr, "%s", PQerrorMessage(conn));
    return -1;
  }

  ntuples = PQntuples(result);
  fprintf(stdout, "%d tuples returns\n", ntuples);

  for (i = 0; i < ntuples; i++)
  {
    char *id, *name;
    int id_col = PQfnumber(result, "id");
    int name_col = PQfnumber(result, "name");
    if (id_col < 0 || name_col < 0)
    {
      fprintf(stderr, "invalid result\n");
      break;
    }
    id = PQgetvalue(result, i, id_col);
    name = PQgetvalue(result, i, name_col);

    fprintf("Data: id = %s, name = %s\n", id, name);
  }

  PQfinish(conn);
  return 0;
}
```

Using status functions

There are some error-handling functions or status functions available to check the results of a function.

Using PQresultStatus

The PQresultStatus function sreturns the status of a command. This function is very important to get the result status after executing the query. This function is the base of the program logic, because a program should take action based on the result status. The syntax for PQtresultStatus is as follows:

```
ExecStatusType PQresultStatus(const PGresult *res);
```

The following is a code snippet to explain the PQresultStatus function:

```
/* Execute a query using PQexec */
result = PQexec(conn, "SELECT id, name FROM foo LIMIT 3");
switch(PQresultStatus(result))
{
  case PGRES_COMMAND_OK:
  /* Query successful and no data to return */
  break;
  case PGRES_TUPLES_OK:
  /* Query ok and data available */
  break;
  case PGRES_EMPTY_QUERY:
  /* Query string was empty */
  break;
  case PGRES_COPY_OUT:
  /* Data transfer from server side started */
  break;
  case PGRES_COPY_IN:
  /* Data transferred started to server */
  break;
  case PGRES_BAD_RESPONSE:
  /* Invalid response from server*/
  break;
  case PGRES_NONFATAL_ERROR:
  /* A notice or warning occurred */
  break;
  case PGRES_FATAL_ERROR:
  /* Fata error occurred. */
  break;
  case PGRES_COPY_BOTH:
```

```
    /* Data transfer start to/from server */
    break;
    default:
    /* Unknown error */
    break;
}
```

Using PQresStatus

This function converts the status code returned by the PQresultStatus function to
a string. The syntax for PQresStatus is as follows:

```
char *PQresStatus(ExecStatusType status);
```

The following code snippet executes a query and gets the status of the result
returned by PQexec using the PQresStatus function:

```
/* Execute a query using PQexec */
result = PQexec(conn, "SELECT id, name FROM foo LIMIT 3");
fprintf(stderr, "failed to execute query: %s\n",
  PQresStatus(PQresultStatus(result)));
failed to execute query: PGRES_FATAL_ERROR
```

By default, libpq is thread safe and PQisthreadsafe can be used to check the status
of thread safety of libpq. The special compiler command-line options should be
used to compile the thread-based application.

Summary

This chapter explains different ways to establish a connection with the PostgreSQL
server and how to specify different options while connecting with database.
Further chapters throw light on how to query a database and manipulate
PostgreSQL data, that is, how to retrieve and insert data into the PostgreSQL server
using the libpq library.

Embedded SQL in C – ECPG

10

The **Embedded C for PostgreSQL (ECPG)** program is a combination of C language and SQL commands. In the previous chapters, we have discussed the SQL commands in detail as well as communication with PostgreSQL in C language. The embedded SQL command is written in the `.pgc` files in the marked section. This is a two-step task:

- The first step is to create a `.pgc` file and compile with ECPG (embedded SQL preprocess). The ECPG program generates a C program
- In the second step, the C program need to be compiled by the standard C compiler

Hence, in this chapter, we will learn how to write the `.pgc` file, and compile it using the ASP and C compilers.

In this chapter, we will learn the following:

- Combining C language with SQL commands
- Constructs of the `.pgc` files
- Different steps to compile the `.pgc` file

Writing ECPG programs

Here is the sample code of the `.pgc` file; we will discuss each and every command in detail in the following sections. This following sample code connects to the PostgreSQL server using ECPG and gets the PostgreSQL version. The code has four parts, the DECLARE section where we can declare the variables and the second part is where we connect to PostgreSQL using the EXEC SQL CONNECT command.

The third part is where we get the version from the PostgreSQL server, and in the fourth and last part we disconnect from the server. The sample code is as follows:

```
/*------------------------------------------------------------
 *
 *ecpg_sample.pgc
 *Get PostgreSQL version using ECPG  *
 *IDENTIFICATION
 *ecpg_sample.c
 *
 *------------------------------------------------------------
 */
#include<stdio.h>
#include<sys/types.h>
#include "libpq-fe.h"
#include "libpq/libpq-fs.h"
#include<stdio.h>
/* 1 - Declare variable version, in the declare section */
EXEC SQL BEGIN DECLARE SECTION;
char version [1024];
EXEC SQL END DECLARE SECTION;

int main (int argc, char **argv)
{
  /* 2 - Connect to PostgreSQL */
  EXEC SQL CONNECT TO postgres AS postgres USER postgres;
  /* 3 - Get the PostgreSQL version information */
  EXEC SQL SELECT version () INTO :version;
  fprintf (stdout, "PostgreSQL Version: %s\n", version);
  /* 4 - Disconnect from PostgreSQL */
  EXEC SQL DISCONNECT ALL;
return 0;
}
```

Compiling an ECPG program

In *Chapter 9, Communicating PostgreSQL Using LibPQ*, we discussed how to compile a C program, but compiling ECPG requires one more step. In the `bin` directory of PostgreSQL, there is an executable program `ecpg`. The `ecpg` program converts a `.pgc` file and creates a `.c` file with the same name. In this example, the ECPG program creates an `ecpg_sample.c` file from an `ecpg_sample.pgc` file.

Execute the ECPG program on the ECPG's `sample.pgc` file to generate the `ecpg_sample.c` file using the following statement:

```
$ ecpg ecpg_sample.pgc
```

List all the files of the current directory, the `ls` command in Linux and the `dir` command in Windows used to list the files using the following statements:

```
$ ls
ecpg_sample.c
ecpg_sample.pgc
```

This `ecpg_sample.c` file can be compiled using a standard C compiler using the following statement:

```
$ make ecpg_sample
```

Run the executable `ecpg_sample` file using the following statement:

```
$ ./ecpg_sample
```

The output of `ecpg_sample` is as follows:

```
$ PostgreSQL Version: PostgreSQL 9.4 on i686-pc-linux-gnu, compiled
  by gcc (Ubuntu 4.8.2-19ubuntu1) 4.8.2, 32-bit
```

> Export LD_LIBRARY_PATH of the `libecpg.so` library
> `# export LD_LIBRARY_PATH=/usr/local/pgsql/lib/`

The following is the `Makefile` to compile the sample code:

```
CC = gcc
POSTGRESQL_INCLUDE = /usr/local/pgsql/include
POSTGRESQL_LIB = /usr/local/pgsql/lib
CFLAGS = -I$(POSTGRESQL_INCLUDE)
LD_FLAGS = -L$(POSTGRESQL_LIB)

all:
    $(CC) ecpg_sample.c -o  ecpg_sample $(CFLAGS)
    $(LD_FLAGS) -lecpg
    $(CC) ecpg_connection.c -o  ecpg_connection $(CFLAGS)
    $(LD_FLAGS) -lecpg
    $(CC) ecpg_prog.c -o  ecpg_prog $(CFLAGS) $(LD_FLAGS) -
    lecpg
    $(CC) ecpg_error.c -o  ecpg_error $(CFLAGS) $(LD_FLAGS)
    -lecpg
    $(CC) ecpg_sqlca.c -o  ecpg_sqlca $(CFLAGS) $(LD_FLAGS)
    -lecpg
    $(CC) ecpg_prep.c -o  ecpg_prep $(CFLAGS) $(LD_FLAGS) -
    lecpg
ecpg_sample:
    $(CC) ecpg_sample.c -o  ecpg_sample $(CFLAGS)
    $(LD_FLAGS) -lecpg
ecpg_connection:
    $(CC) ecpg_connection.c -o  ecpg_connection $(CFLAGS)
    $(LD_FLAGS) -lecpg
ecpg_prog:
    $(CC) ecpg_prog.c -o  ecpg_prog $(CFLAGS) $(LD_FLAGS) -
    lecpg
ecpg_error:
    $(CC) ecpg_error.c -o  ecpg_error $(CFLAGS) $(LD_FLAGS)
    -lecpg
ecpg_sqlca:
    $(CC) ecpg_sqlca.c -o  ecpg_sqlca $(CFLAGS) $(LD_FLAGS)
    -lecpg
ecpg_prep:
    $(CC) ecpg_prep.c -o  ecpg_prep $(CFLAGS) $(LD_FLAGS) -
    lecpg
clean:
    rm -rf *.o
    ecpg_sample ecpg_connection ecpg_prog ecpg_error ecpg_sqlca
    ecpg_prep
```

 Do not edit a .c file because it is a generated file, and your edit will be lost.

ECPG DECLARE sections

While writing a `.pgc` program, we need to declare sections to write an SQL command. All SQL variables that will be used will need to be declared between the `BEGIN` and `END` `DECLARE` section as follows:

```
EXEC SQL BEGIN DECLARE SECTION;
/* Declare SQL Variables */
EXEC SQL END DECLARE SECTION;
```

Connection using ECPG

The `CONNECT` command is used to connect to the PostgreSQL server. Its syntax is as follows:

```
EXEC SQL CONNECT TO target [AS connection-name] [USER user-name];
```

Let's consider the parameters of the preceding syntax:

- `target`: The target PostgreSQL system includes information about the host system, port information, connection options and database name as shown:

  ```
  [tcp/unix]:postgresql://hostname [:port]/dbname[?options]
  ```

  For example, if we want to connect a local instance of PostgreSQL using `tcp`, we will use the following target:

  ```
  tcp:postgresql://127.0.01:5432/testdb
  ```

- `connection-name`: This is the name of the connection. In some cases, the program needs to make multiple connections with the database. Therefore, this connection parameter is used to identify the connection. This is an optional parameter, as in some cases the program does not need to have multiple connections with the database

- `user`: This option is used to specify the username and the password and can be in multiple formats such as the following:

  ```
  EXEC SQL CONNECT TO postgres USER username / password;
  EXEC SQL CONNECT TO postgres USER username IDENTIFIED BY
    password;
  EXEC SQL CONNECT TO postgres USER username USING password;
  ```

Disconnecting using ECPG

The SQL DISCONNECT command is used to disconnect from the server. This command can disconnect from current, default, and all sessions. Its syntax is as follows:

```
EXEC SQL DISCONNECT [connection];
```

Here connection is the name of the connection to disconnect. It can be the connection name, DEFAULT, CURRENT, or ALL.

Selecting a connection

We have already discussed that we can create multiple connections with the database in ECPG. There is a way to select connections too. ECPG provides multiple ways to select the connection.

One way is to switch between the connections using the connection name. In this case, the connection is switched and all the SQL commands will use that connection. The syntax of the SET CONNECTION statement is as follows:

```
EXEC SQL SET CONNECTION connection-name;
```

Here connection-name is the name of the connection, as we provided while connecting with PostgreSQL.

The other way is to explicitly select a connection for each and every SQL command as follows:

```
EXEC SQL AT connection-name SQL command;
```

Here is an example of a pgc program to establish multiple connections with PostgreSQL using ECPG. The following code used Unix domain sockets and a TCP variant to connect to PostgreSQL:

```
/*-----------------------------------------------------------------
 *
 *connection.pgc
 *Connecting PostgreSQL Server using ecpg
 *
 *IDENTIFICATION
 *connection.pgc
 *
 *-----------------------------------------------------------------
 */
#include<stdio.h>
```

```
#include<sys/types.h>
#include<stdio.h>
EXEC SQL BEGIN DECLARE SECTION;
  chartarget_tcp[] = "tcp:postgresql://127.0.01:5432/postgres";
  chartarget_unix[] = "unix:postgresql://localhost:5432/postgres";
  char *version;
EXEC SQL END DECLARE SECTION;

int main(int argc, char **argv)
{
  /* Establish connection using TCP */
  EXEC SQL CONNECT TO :target_tcp AS connection_tcp USER postgres;
  /* Establish connection using Unix domain socket */
  EXEC SQL CONNECT TO :target_unix AS connection_unix USER
  postgres;
  /* Run the command using target_tcp connection */
  EXEC SQL AT connection_tcp SELECT version() INTO :version;
  fprintf(stdout, "PostgreSQL Version Using UNIX domain socket:
  %s\n", version);
  /* Switch connection to target_unix */
  EXEC SQL SET CONNECTION connection_unix;
  fprintf(stdout, "PostgreSQL Version Using TCP: %s\n", version);
  /* Disconnect connection_tcp connection */
  EXEC SQL DISCONNECT connection_tcp;
  /* Disconnect all will close the connection_unix which is still
  open */
  EXEC SQL DISCONNECT ALL;
  return 0;
}
```

 You do not need to include ecpglib.h in your pgc program. The ECPG program will add the ECPG header files in generated .c file.

Running SQL commands

We have discussed how to connect to the PostgreSQL server using ECPG. After connection, we can run the SQL commands. This command can be a DDL or DML statement. The syntax to run SQL commands on the PostgreSQL server is as follows:

```
EXEC SQL sql_command
```

Here is the complete example to drop a table, create a table, insert/update/delete data, and use the cursor to fetch the data. The syntax of SQL commands is the same as we have discussed in previous chapters in detail.

```
/*-----------------------------------------------------------------
 *
 *ecpg_prog.pgc
 *Connecting PostgreSQL Server using ecpg
 *
 *IDENTIFICATION
 *ecpg_prog.pgc
 *
 *-----------------------------------------------------------------
 */
#include <stdio.h>
#include <sys/types.h>
#include <stdio.h>

EXEC SQL BEGIN DECLARE SECTION;
  char target[] = "unix:postgresql://localhost:5432/postgres";
  int id;
  char name[255];
EXEC SQL END DECLARE SECTION;

int main(int argc, char **argv)
{
  EXEC SQL CONNECT TO :target AS connection_unix USER postgres;
  /* Drop table */
  EXEC SQL DROP TABLE IF EXISTS foo;
  /* Create table foo */
  EXEC SQL CREATE TABLE foo (id INTEGER, name TEXT);
  /* Insert data into table foo */
  EXEC SQL INSERT INTO foo VALUES (1, 'foo1');
  EXEC SQL INSERT INTO foo VALUES (2, 'foo2');
  EXEC SQL INSERT INTO foo VALUES (3, 'foo3');
  /* Selecting data from table foo */
  EXEC SQL SELECT id, name FROM foo LIMIT 1;
  /* Selecting data from table using cursor */
  EXEC SQL DECLARE cur CURSOR FOR SELECT id, name FROM foo WHERE
  id = 3;
  EXEC SQL OPEN cur;
  EXEC SQL FETCH cur INTO :id, :name;
  EXEC SQL CLOSE cur;
  EXEC SQL COMMIT;
```

```
fprintf(stdout, "Fetch from cursor: Id = %d, Name = %s\n", id,
name);
/* Update table foo */
EXEC SQL UPDATE foo SET id = 4 WHERE id = 3;
/* Delete from table foo */
EXEC SQL DELETE FROM foo WHERE id = 1;
/* Disconnect all connections, this will close the
connection_unix which is still open */
EXEC SQL DISCONNECT ALL;
return 0;
}
```

Using host variables

Normally, in programs, we don't execute static SQL statements to execute. We need a way where we can pass variables to SQL statements and get the value in C programs. ECPG provides a concept called **host variables** to achieve this.

Passing values to SQL

The : symbol is used for the host variables. In this example, there are two host variables, id and name, that are used to insert the data. The values of variable id and name will be passed to the INSERT statement in the following manner:

```
EXEC SQL INSERT INTO foo VALUES (:id, :name);
```

Getting values from SQL

In the following example, we are passing the variable with :, but this time for getting the values from the SELECT statement. The SELECT statement sets the result into the id and name variables as follows:

```
EXEC SQL SELECT id, name INTO :id, :name FROM foo;
```

We need to pass a second host variable to get the null value of the column, otherwise an error will occur in case of the null value. This can be done in the following manner:

```
EXEC SELECT id FROM foo INTO :id :id_ind;
```

Dynamic SQL

ECPG also supports prepared statements. In ECPG, we can prepare the query first and then execute it. This can be seen in the following example:

```
/*----------------------------------------------------------------
 *
 *ecpg_prep.pgc
 *Communicating PostgreSQL Server using ECPG
 *
 *IDENTIFICATION
 *ecpg_prep.pgc
 *
 *----------------------------------------------------------------
 */
#include<stdio.h>
#include<sys/types.h>
#include<stdio.h>

EXEC SQL BEGIN DECLARE SECTION;
  char target[] = "unix:postgresql://localhost:5432/postgres";
  const char *stmt = "INSERT INTO foo VALUES(?, ?);";
  int id;
  char name[255];
EXEC SQL END DECLARE SECTION;

int main(int argc, char **argv)
{
  id = 1;
  fprintf(name, "%s", "bar");
  EXEC SQL CONNECT TO :target AS connection_unix USER postgres;
  /* Drop table */
  EXEC SQL DROP TABLE IF EXISTS foo;
  /* Create table foo */
  EXEC SQL CREATE TABLE foo (id INTEGER, name TEXT);
  /* Insert values using Prepared statement */
  EXEC SQL WHENEVER SQLERROR SQLPRINT;
  EXEC SQL PREPARE prepared_stmtFROM :stmt;
  /* Using Host variable to insert value */
  EXEC SQL EXECUTE prepared_stmtUSING :id, :name;
  EXEC SQL COMMIT;
  EXEC SQL DISCONNECT ALL;
  return 0;
}
```

Error handling

ECPG provides multiple mechanisms to handle exceptional conditions and warnings. The following are the mechanisms used for error handling:

- Setting callback using the WHENEVER statement
- Using the sqlca variable to check for detailed information about the error and warning

How to set an error callback

The WHENEVER command is used to set the condition and action. The actions are called when the condition is met. The syntax for the WHENEVER statement is as follows:

```
EXEC SQL WHENEVER condition action;
```

Conditions

There are three conditions we can specify in the WHENEVER conditions: SQLERROR, SQLWARNING, and NOT FOUND. Let's understand them one by one:

- SQLERROR: This condition arises if an error occurs while executing the SQL statement. Its syntax is as follows:

```
EXEC SQL WHENEVER SQLERROR GOTO error_label;
```

- SQLWARNING: This condition arises if a warning occurs while executing the SQL statement. Its syntax is as follows:

```
EXEC SQL WHENEVER SQLWARNING GOTO warning_label;
```

- NOT FOUND: This condition arises if there is no or zero row found. Its syntax is as follows:

```
EXEC SQL WHENEVER NOT FOUND GOTO no_more_rows_label;
```

NOT FOUND is not an error condition, but this is an important information for the program.

The error_label, warning_label, and no_more_label are C language labels.

Actions

After specifying the condition, we need to specify the action. There are many actions we can specify in the WHENEVER statement. These actions occur when one of these, SQLERROR, SQLWARNING, or NOT FOUND, conditions are met. Let's consider the following actions:

- CONTINUE: This action means do nothing and ignore the condition
- GOTO label: This action means to jump to the defined label (labels is a C code label)
- GO TO label: This is a synonym of GOTO
- SQLPRINT: This action prints the error message
- STOP: This action terminates the program using EXIT (1)
- DOBREAK: This action breaks the loop or SWITCH statement; it is done using the C programming's BREAK statement
- CALL name (args): This action calls the C function
- DO name (args): This is a synonym of CALL

Here is a detailed example of the preceding discussed conditions and actions (the code branch and the code based on WHENEVER conditions).

First the code captures the SQLERROR condition and prints the error as follows:

```
EXEC SQL WHENEVER SQLERROR SQLPRINT;
```

After this code, capture SQLERROR again and jump to the C label ERROR_LABEL as follows:

```
EXEC SQL WHENEVER SQLERROR GOTO error_label;
```

Consider the following example, which uses the preceding discussed conditions and actions:

```
/*-------------------------------------------------------------
 *
 *ecpg_error.pgc
 *Communicating PostgreSQL Server using ECPG
 *
 *IDENTIFICATION
 *ecpg_error.pgc
 *
 *-------------------------------------------------------------
 */
```

```
#include<stdio.h>
#include<sys/types.h>
#include<stdio.h>

EXEC SQL BEGIN DECLARE SECTION;
  char target[] = "unix:postgresql://localhost:5432/postgres";
  int id;
  char name[255];
EXEC SQL END DECLARE SECTION;

int main(int argc, char **argv)
{
  EXEC SQL CONNECT TO: target AS connection_unix USER postgres;
  /* Drop table */
  EXEC SQL DROP TABLE IF EXISTS foo;
  /* Create table foo */
  EXEC SQL CREATE TABLE foo (id INTEGER, name TEXT);
/*
 * Try to insert wrong number of columns
 * into table to produce error and capture
 * the error using SQLERROR "condition and
 * perform SQLPRINT action.
 */
  EXEC SQL WHENEVER SQLERROR SQLPRINT;
  EXEC SQL INSERT INTO foo VALUES (1, 2, 'foo1');
  EXEC SQL COMMIT;
/*
 * Try to insert wrong number of columns
 * into table to produce error and capture
 * the error using SQLERROR "condition and
 * perform GOTO action.
 */
  EXEC SQL WHENEVER SQLERROR GOTO error_label;
  EXEC SQL INSERT INTO foo VALUES (1, 2, 'foo1');
  EXEC SQL COMMIT;
  EXEC SQL DISCONNECT ALL;
  return 0;

  error_label:
  fprintf(stderr, "\nSQL Error occur and captured using SQLERROR
condition\n");
  EXEC SQL DISCONNECT ALL;
  return 1;
```

```
WARNING_LABEL:
fprintf(stderr, "\nSQL WARNING occur and captured using
SQLWARNING condition\n");
EXEC SQL DISCONNECT ALL;
return 1;
}
```

Using sqlca for error handling

SQL Communication Area (sqlca) is a C structure and can be used to get the detailed information about the error.

The structure is as follows:

```
struct
{
  charsqlcaid[8];
  longsqlabc;
  longsqlcode;
  struct
  {
    intsqlerrml;
    charsqlerrmc[SQLERRMC_LEN];
  } sqlerrm;
  charsqlerrp[8];
  longsqlerrd[6];
  charsqlwarn[8];
  charsqlstate[5];
} sqlca;
```

Here is the complete example of ECPG program to print the detailed information about the error-like code and error message. The `print_sqlca()` function prints every field of the `sqlca` structure. In case of `SQLERROR` and `print_sqlca()` function will be called and will print the details of error as follows:

```
EXEC SQL WHENEVER SQLERROR CALL print_sqlca();
```

The following example shows detailed information about the error-like code and error messages:

```
/*-------------------------------------------------------------
 *
 *ecpg_sqlca.pgc
 *Communicating PostgreSQL Server using ECPG
 *
```

```
 *IDENTIFICATION
 *ecpg_sqlca.pgc
 *
 *--------------------------------------------------------------
 */
#include<stdio.h>
#include<sys/types.h>
#include<stdio.h>

EXEC SQL BEGIN DECLARE SECTION;
  char target[] = "unix:postgresql://localhost:5432/postgres";
  int id;
  char name[255];
EXEC SQL END DECLARE SECTION;

/* Reference: http://www.postgresql.org/docs/9.4/static/ecpg-errors.
html */
void
print_sqlca()
{
  fprintf(stderr, "==== sqlca ====\n");
  fprintf(stderr, "sqlcode: %ld\n", sqlca.sqlcode);
  fprintf(stderr, "sqlerrm.sqlerrml: %d\n",
  sqlca.sqlerrm.sqlerrml);
  fprintf(stderr, "sqlerrm.sqlerrmc: %s\n",
  sqlca.sqlerrm.sqlerrmc);
  fprintf(stderr, "sqlerrd: %ld %ld %ld %ld %ld %ld\n",
  sqlca.sqlerrd[0],sqlca.sqlerrd[1],sqlca.sqlerrd[2],
  sqlca.sqlerrd[3],sqlca.sqlerrd[4],sqlca.sqlerrd[5]);
  fprintf(stderr, "sqlwarn: %d %d %d %d %d %d %d %d\n",
  sqlca.sqlwarn[0], sqlca.sqlwarn[1], sqlca.sqlwarn[2],
  sqlca.sqlwarn[3], sqlca.sqlwarn[4], sqlca.sqlwarn[5],
  sqlca.sqlwarn[6], sqlca.sqlwarn[7]);
  fprintf(stderr, "sqlstate: %5s\n", sqlca.sqlstate);
  fprintf(stderr, "===============\n");
}
int main(int argc, char **argv)
{
  EXEC SQL CONNECT TO :target AS connection_unix USER postgres;
  /* Drop table */
  EXEC SQL DROP TABLE IF EXISTS foo;
  /* Create table foo */
  EXEC SQL CREATE TABLE foo (id INTEGER, name TEXT);
  EXEC SQL WHENEVER SQLERROR CALL print_sqlca();
```

```
    EXEC SQL INSERT INTO foo VALUES (1, 2, 'foo1');
    EXEC SQL COMMIT;
    EXEC SQL DISCONNECT ALL;
    return 0;
}
```

The output of the program is as follows:

```
==== sqlca ====
sqlcode: -400
sqlerrm.sqlerrml: 58
sqlerrm.sqlerrmc: INSERT has more expressions than target columns
    on line 52
sqlerrd: 0 00000
sqlwarn: 0 0000000
sqlstate: 42601
===============
```

Summary

In this chapter, we have discussed what ECPG is and how to write SQL commands mixed with C code. We also elaborated on how to establish a connection with the PostgreSQL server using ECPG, how to run SQL commands, and how to handle error and warning conditions.

In the next chapter, we will learn the concept of foreign data wrappers and about the two communities maintaining foreign data wrappers file_fdw and postgres_fdw.

11
Foreign Data Wrapper

PostgreSQL 9.1 has a new feature called **Foreign Data Wrapper** (**FDW**). A foreign data wrapper is a template to write the module to access foreign data. This is based on the **SQL/MED (SQL/Management of External Data)** standard. The SQL/MED was added to the SQL standard in 2003. This is a standard to access remote objects from SQL.

Only `postgres_fdw` and `file_fdw` are officially maintained foreign data wrappers and part of the PostgreSQL's `contrib` modules. In this chapter, we will learn how to use `postgres_fdw` and `file_fdw` in detail.

There are many foreign data wrappers available and we can find the complete list from the following site:

`https://wiki.postgresql.org/wiki/Foreign_data_wrappers`.

In this chapter, we will learn about the following:

- How to create a server, user mapping, and foreign tables
- Implementing foreign data wrappers in PostgreSQL

Creating foreign data wrappers

PostgreSQL uses the following syntax for creating foreign data wrappers:

```
CREATE FOREIGN DATA WRAPPER name
    [ HANDLER handler_function | NO HANDLER ]
    [ VALIDATOR validator_function | NO VALIDATOR ]
    [ OPTIONS ( option 'value' [, ... ] ) ]
```

Let's consider the various parameters mentioned in the preceding syntax:

- `name`: This is the name of the foreign data wrapper to be created.

- `HANDLER handler_function`: The `handler_function` is called to retrieve the execution function. The return type of the function must be `fdw_handler`.

 A foreign data wrapper without `handler_function` cannot be accessed.

- `VALIDATOR validator_function`: The foreign data wrapper has functionality where we can provide a generic option while creating the server, user mapping, and foreign data wrapper. The `validator_function` is called to validate these generic options. If there is no validator function specified, then the option will not be checked.

 Only a superuser can create foreign data wrappers.

The basic components of foreign data wrappers

A PostgreSQL foreign data wrapper consists of many components. We are going to explain them in detail, starting with the C file.

The C file

There is a need for a C programming source code file that will contain the implementation of `handler_function` and `validator_function`. The C programming source should define the handler and validator function as follows:

```
extern Datum dummy_fdw_handler (PG_FUNCTION_ARGS);
extern Datum dummy_fdw_validator (PG_FUNCTION_ARGS);
PG_FUNCTION_INFO_V1 (dummy_fdw_handler);
PG_FUNCTION_INFO_V1 (dummy_fdw_validator);
```

The `handler_function` function, which is `dummy_fdw_handler` in the given example, should return the `FdwRoutine` structure pointer. The `FdwRoutine` structure contains the pointer of implementation call-back functions. The foreign data wrapper calls the functions using these `FdwRoutine` function pointers.

The foreign data wrapper machinery will not call any function whose pointer is null. This can be seen in the following example:

```
FdwRoutine *dummy_fdw_handler(PG_FUNCTION_ARGS)
{
  FdwRoutine *fdwroutine = makeNode (FdwRoutine);

  /* Callback functions for readable FDW */
  fdwroutine->GetForeignRelSize = dummyGetForeignRelSize;
  fdwroutine->GetForeignPaths = dummyGetForeignPaths;
  fdwroutine->AnalyzeForeignTable = dummyAnalyzeForeignTable;
  fdwroutine->GetForeignPlan = dummyGetForeignPlan;
  fdwroutine->ExplainForeignScan = dummyExplainForeignScan;
  fdwroutine->BeginForeignScan = dummyBeginForeignScan;
  fdwroutine->IterateForeignScan = dummyIterateForeignScan;
  fdwroutine->ReScanForeignScan = dummyReScanForeignScan;
  fdwroutine->EndForeignScan = dummyEndForeignScan;

  /* Callback functions for writeable FDW */
  fdwroutine->ExecForeignInsert = dummyExecForeignInsert;
  fdwroutine->BeginForeignModify = dummyBeginForeignModify;
  fdwroutine->PlanForeignModify = dummyPlanForeignModify;
  fdwroutine->AddForeignUpdateTargets =
    dummyAddForeignUpdateTargets;
  fdwroutine->ExecForeignUpdate = dummyExecForeignUpdate;
  fdwroutine->ExecForeignDelete = dummyExecForeignDelete;
  fdwroutine->EndForeignModify = dummyEndForeignModify;

  PG_RETURN_POINTER(fdwroutine);
}
```

Another important thing is a validator function that is responsible for validation of the CREATE SERVER, CREATE USER MAPPING, and CREATE FOREIGN TABLE options. Its syntax is as follows:

```
Datum dummy_fdw_validator(PG_FUNCTION_ARGS)
{
}
```

Makefile to compile the foreign data wrapper

As we have already discussed that we need the C programming source code file for implementation, we now need a `Makefile` to compile the source code to generate a library. Here is the sample `Makefile` to compile the `dummy_fdw` foreign data wrapper:

```
# Makefile
MODULE_big = dummy_fdw
OBJS = dummy_fdw.o
EXTENSION = dummy_fdw
DATA = dummy_fdw--1.0.sql
REGRESS = dummy_fdw

DUMMY_CONFIG = dummy_config
subdir = contrib/dummy_fdw
top_builddir = ../..
include $(top_builddir)/src/Makefile.global
include $(top_srcdir)/contrib/contrib-global.mk
```

Let's consider the various parameters mentioned in the preceding snippet:

* `MODULE_big`: This is the name of the module
* `OBJS`: This is the C source code file for compilation
* `DATA`: This is the name of SQL file. For details see the following section
* `REGRESS`: This is the the regression file name

A SQL file to map SQL functions to C functions

A SQL file is needed to map the C handler and validate function to the SQL function. It not only maps the C function with the SQL function, but also creates a foreign data wrapper using the CREATE FOREIGN DATA WRAPPER command in the following manner:

```
-- File name=dummy_fdw--1.0.sql
CREATE FUNCTION dummy_fdw_handler()
RETURNS fdw_handler
AS 'MODULE_PATHNAME'
LANGUAGE C STRICT;

CREATE FUNCTION dummy_fdw_validator(text[], oid)
RETURNS void
AS 'MODULE_PATHNAME'
```

```
LANGUAGE C STRICT;

CREATE FOREIGN DATA WRAPPER dummy_fdw
  HANDLER dummy_fdw_handler
  VALIDATOR dummy_fdw_validator;
```

The control file to manage version and module path

A module or extension control file contains the wrapper version and module library path as shown:

```
#dummy_fdw.control
comment = 'Foreign data wrapper for querying a dummy server'
default_version = '1.0'
module_pathname = '$libdir/dummy_fdw'
relocatable = true
```

Let's consider the various parameters mentioned in the preceding snippet:

- comment: This gives the comments for the foreign data wrapper
- default_version: This gives the version number of extension
- Module_pathname: This gives the foreign data wrapper library path

Loading foreign data wrappers

Foreign data wrappers are extensions and can be loaded using CREATE EXTENSION. We will discuss extensions in the next chapter in detail. The syntax for loading foreign data wrappers is as follows:

```
CREATE EXTENION dummy_fdw;
```

Creating a server

After loading the extension, we need to create a foreign server that typically consists of connection information. Normally, the connection information consists of a remote machine hostname or IP address and target system port number. The user information may be specified in user mapping.

```
CREATE SERVER server_name
  [ TYPE 'server_type' ] [ VERSION 'server_version' ]
  FOREIGN DATA WRAPPER fdw_name
  [ OPTIONS ( option 'value' [, ... ] ) ]
```

Let's consider the various parameters mentioned in the preceding syntax:

- `server_name`: This is the name of the server. This will be referred while creating the foreign tables.
- `server_type`: This is the type of the server. This is optional.
- `server_version`: This is the server version information; it This is optional.
- `fdw_name`: This is the name of the foreign data wrapper.
- OPTIONS: This is the optional server specific information, normally contains the connection information. These options are validated in `dummy_fdw` validator.

The following statement creates a server named `dummy_server` of the `dummy_fdw` foreign data wrapper:

```
CREATE SERVER dummy_server FOREIGN DATA WRAPPER dummy_fdw;
```

Creating user mapping

The connection information consists of two parts; one is the target address, for example, host name, IP address ,and port; and the second part is the user information. The CREATE SERVER statement covers the target address part and CREATE USER MAPPING covers the user information part. The CREATE USER MAPPING statement mapped the PostgreSQL user to the foreign server user. The syntax for CREATE USER MAPPING is as follows:

```
CREATE USER MAPPING FOR
  { user_name | USER | CURRENT_USER | PUBLIC }
  SERVER server_name
  [ OPTIONS ( option 'value' [ , ... ] ) ]
```

Let's consider the various parameters mentioned in the preceding syntax:

- `user_name`: This is the name of the existing PostgreSQL user that needs to be mapped. The CURRENT_USER and USER parameter means the current logged in user, and PUBLIC is used when no user specific mapping is required.
- `server_name`: This is the name of the server for which user mapping is required.
- OPTIONS: These are the foreign data wrapper dependent options. Normally it contains the remote or foreign server username and password.

Here is a simple example to create user mapping for the `postgres` user:

```
CREATE USER MAPPING FOR postgres SERVER dummy_server
  OPTIONS(username 'foo', password 'bar');
```

Creating a foreign table

After creating the server and user mapping, the next step is to create a foreign table. The syntax for creating a foreign table is as follows:

```
CREATE FOREIGN TABLE [ IF NOT EXISTS ] table_name
  ( [column_namedata_type
  [ OPTIONS ( option 'value' [, ... ] ) ]
  [ COLLATE collation ]
  [ column_constraint [ ... ] ] [, ... ] ] )
  SERVER server_name [ OPTIONS ( option 'value' [, ... ] ) ]
WHERE column_constraint is:
[ CONSTRAINT constraint_name ]
{ NOT NULL | NULL | DEFAULT default_expr }
```

Let's consider the various parameters mentioned in the preceding syntax:

- `table_name`: This is the name of the table.
- `column_name`: This is the name of the column.
- `data_type`: This gives the data type.
- `DEFAULT default_expr`: This is the the `DEFAULT` clause.
- `server_name`: This is the name of the foreign server.
- `OPTIONS`: This is the foreign data wrapper specific table options. It normally contains the remote table name.

Here is a simple example to create a user mapping for the `postgres` user:

```
CREATE FOREIGN TABLE dummy_table
  (
  id INTEGER,
  name TEXT
  )
  SERVER dummy_server OPTIONS(table_name 'remote_dummy_table');
```

 Creating a foreign table is remote mapping a table and does not mean creating a table on a remote server. It is a mapped table on a remote server.

Using foreign data wrappers

After creating the foreign table, we can perform DML on the table just like a normal table like the following statement:

```
SELECT * FROM dummy_table;
```

Working with postgres_fdw

PostgreSQL provides a template to create your own foreign data wrapper, and there are many foreign data wrappers available on the Internet. But there are only two officially supported foreign data wrappers: postgres_fdw and file_fdw. The postgres_fdw is a foreign data wrapper that is used to retrieve and manipulate the remote PostgreSQL's server. The postgres_fdw data wrapper can be used by performing the following steps:

1. Load the extension using CREATE EXTENSION:

    ```
    postgres=# CREATE EXTENSION postgres_fdw;
    ```

2. Create the server using CREATE SERVER:

    ```
    postgres=# CREATE SERVER postgres_server FOREIGN DATA
               WRAPPER postgres_fdw OPTIONS (host, '127.0.0.1',
               port '5432', dbname 'postgres');
    ```

3. Create user mapping using CREATE USER MAPPING:

    ```
    postgres=# CREATE USER MAPPING FOR PUBLIC SERVER
               postgres_server;
    ```

4. Create a foreign table using CREATE FOREIGN TABLE:

    ```
    postgres=# CREATE FOREIGN TABLE dummy_table (foo INTEGER,
               bar TEXT) SERVER postgres_server OPTIONS
               (table_name 'remote_dummy_table');
    ```

5. Insert data into the foreign table:

    ```
    postgres=# INSERT INTO dummy_table VALUES (1, 'foo');
    ```

6. Select data from the foreign data wrapper:

    ```
    postgres=# SELECT * FROM dummy_table;
     foo | bar
    -----+-----
    (0 rows)
    ```

Working with file_fdw

The file_fdw data wrapper is another officially supported foreign data wrapper. This is used to access the files in the server file system. The file_fdw data wrapper can be used by performing the following steps:

1. Load extension using CREATE EXTENSION:

    ```
    postgres=# CREATE EXTENSION file_fdw;
    ```

2. Create the server using CREATE SERVER:

   ```
   postgres=# CREATE SERVER file_svr FOREIGN DATA WRAPPER
              file_fdw;
   ```

3. Create a foreign table using CREATE FOREIGN TABLE:

   ```
   postgres=# CREATE FOREIGN TABLE logfile
      (log_id INTEGER,
      log_detail TEXT,
      log_date date)
      SERVER file_svr
      OPTIONS (filename, 'log.txt', delimiter ',');
   ```

The log.txt file contains one record per line and every field is separated by a comma; in other words, log.txt is a **Comma Separated File (CSF)**.

> The contents of the log.txt file are:
> ```
> $ cat log.txt
> 1. Unable to open file, 01/12/2014
> 2. Parsing error , 02/01/2014
> 3. Initialization failed, 02/01/2014
> ```

Selecting the data from a foreign server will show the contents of the log.txt file:

```
postgres=# SELECT * FROM logfile;
 log_id |          log_detail           log_date
--------+-----------------------------------------
      1 | Unable to open file        2014-12-01
      2 | Parsing error'             2014-01-02
      3 | Initialization failed      2014-01-02
(3 rows)
```

Summary

In this chapter, we learned what a foreign data wrapper is, how to create a foreign data wrapper and how to use existing foreign data wrappers. We have also learned postgres_fdw and file_fdw in detail.

In the next chapter, we will learn what an extension is and how to create extensions and how to use existing extensions.

12
Extensions

While using PostgreSQL, the user may feel the need to expand certain PostgreSQL functionalities by including multiple SQL objects, like new operators, new index operator classes, and new data types along with new functions. In PostgreSQL, all these objects are collected into a single package called **extension**. When creating an extension, a user will need to have the following files:

- A SQL script file, which must have some SQL commands for creating objects
- A `control` file, which specifies a few basic properties of the extension
- If the extension includes C code, then there will be a C shared `library` file

After getting all these files in one place, the user can create the extension by simply using the SQL command `CREATE EXTENSION extension_name`. The `CREATE EXTENSION` command will load objects present in the extension into the current database.

We will learn the following in the upcoming sections:

- What an extension is
- How to `CREATE`, `ALTER`, and `DELETE` an extension
- PostgreSQL supplied extensions

Features of an extension

There are many features of extensions and the most important feature is *ease of use*. The user can simply load all objects in the database with the single `CREATE EXTENSION` command and can drop all the objects with a single `DROP EXTENSION` command. When the object is enclosed inside the extension, PostgreSQL will not allow any user to drop an individual object contained in an extension; the only way to achieve this goal is by dropping the whole extension.

The user can modify the definition of an extension member object by utilizing the feature of a superseding command for member objects. The extension in addition has a procedure for packaging the modified SQL objects contained in an extension. Consider this example; if the second version of an extension integrates one function and changes the body of another function compared to the first version, then the extension owner can provide an updated script that makes just those two changes. The user can utilize the `ALTER EXTENSION` command to apply these changes and track which version of the extension is authentically installed in a given database.

Extensions can have different types of PostgreSQL objects like functions and tables, but the database, table space and roles cannot be part of the extension. Extensions are valid only within the database in which they are created. A table can be a member of an extension, but indexes on tables are not considered members of the extension. Another thing to keep in mind is that schemas can belong to extensions, but extensions cannot belong to schemas because an extension does not subsist within any schema. The extension's member objects, however, will belong to schemas whenever appropriate for their object types. It may or may not be appropriate for an extension to own the schema its member objects are within.

There are many advantages of the extensions, and a few of them are extensively repeatability and extension update. The user can update the extension easily as PostgreSQL provides an easy way to manage updates to the SQL commands that define an extension object. Updates can be performed by giving a version name for each version of the extension's install script. On the other hand, if users want to update databases dynamically from one version to the next version, then the user should utilize the update scripts that make the essential changes to go from one version to the next. The update scripts have names with the following pattern:

```
extension--oldversion--newversion.sql
```

The following is an example of the preceding pattern:

```
tempext--1.0--1.1.sql
```

The preceding SQL file contains the SQL commands to change the `temp` extension from `1.0` to `1.1`. When an updated script is available, the user/developer can use the following command:

```
ALTER EXTENSION UPDATE
```

This command will update an installed extension to the specific revision. The `ALTER EXTENSION` command can execute sequences of update script files to perform a requested update. For example, if only `tempext--1.0--1.1.sql` and `tempext--1.1--2.0.sql` are available, then the `ALTER EXTENSION` command will be applied to them in sequence if an update to version 2.0 is requested when 1.0 is currently installed.

Creating extensions

When creating an extension that is shipped to the PostgreSQL installer, users uses the CREATE EXTENSION command as follows:

```
CREATE EXTENSION [IF NOT EXISTS] extension_name
  [WITH] [SCHEMA schema_name]
  [Version]
  [FROM old_version]
```

When the user calls the CREATE EXTENSION command, it will load a specified extension into the current database. There must not be an extension of the same name already loaded. If an extension with the same name is already loaded, the user will get an error. In the backend, when the user calls the LOAD EXTENSION command, the extension script file will be executed. The script will create initial SQL objects that are mainly functions, data types, operators, and indexes. The CREATE EXTENSION command, in addition, notes down the identities of all the created objects so that they can be dropped again later, if the user executes the DROP EXTENSION command. Only superusers or users who have database owner privileges can create or drop an extension. Moreover, the user who runs the command of creating an extension will own the extension. Let's go through the details of each parameter that we mentioned in the preceding command:

- IF NOT EXISTS: The IF NOT EXISTS statement, when used, tells PostgreSQL to not throw an error if an extension with the same name already exists. If it exists, only a notice is issued.

- extension_name: The extension_name parameter is the name of the extension to be installed. The PostgreSQL will create the extension using details from the control file. Control files are normally present at the sharedir/extension/extension_name.control location.

- schema_name: The schema_name parameter represents the name of the schema in which users wishes to install the extension's objects, given that the extension allows its contents to be relocated. When specifying the schema name, it must be present in the same database. If the user does not give a schema name, then the default object creation schema is used.

 You can view a list of schemas in the current path by using this command:
```
# show search_path;
```

- `Version`: The `Version` parameter shows the version of the extension to be installed. The default version is whatever is specified in the extension's `control` file.

- `old_version`: From the `old_version` parameter, this must be specified when you are trying to install an extension that replaces an *old style* module, which is a collection of objects not packaged into an extension.

> The extensions currently available for loading can be verified by using the following command:
>
> `SELECT * FROM pg_available_extensions;`

Let's install the `adminpack` extension into the current database:

```
warehouse_db=# CREATE EXTENSION adminpack;
```

The preceding command will create an `adminpack` extension in your current schema.

Altering extensions

In most cases, more than one version of the extension is available; the user can install any version as per his requirement. The user can update the extension from older versions to newer versions. The `ALTER EXTENSION` command is the only way to update extensions from one version to another version. The `ALTER` command changes the definition of an existing extension. The `ALTER EXTENSION` command supports the following variation:

```
ALTER EXTENSION extension_name UPDATE [ TO new_version ]
ALTER EXTENSION extension_name SET SCHEMA new_schema
ALTER EXTENSION extension_name ADD member_object
ALTER EXTENSION extension_name DROP member_object
```

In the preceding commands, the `member_object` parameter is:

```
AGGREGATE aggregate_name ( aggregate_signature ) |
CAST (source_type AS target_type) |
COLLATION object_name |
CONVERSION object_name |
DOMAIN object_name |
EVENT TRIGGER object_name |
FOREIGN DATA WRAPPER object_name |
FOREIGN TABLE object_name |
FUNCTION function_name ( [ [ argmode ] [ argname ] argtype [, ...]
    ] ) |
```

```
MATERIALIZED VIEW object_name |
OPERATOR operator_name (left_type, right_type) |
OPERATOR CLASS object_name USING index_method |
OPERATOR FAMILY object_name USING index_method |
[PROCEDURAL ] LANGUAGE object_name |
SCHEMA object_name |
SEQUENCE object_name |
SERVER object_name |
TABLE object_name |
TEXT SEARCH CONFIGURATION object_name |
TEXT SEARCH DICTIONARY object_name |
TEXT SEARCH PARSER object_name |
TEXT SEARCH TEMPLATE object_name |
TYPE object_name |
VIEW object_name
```

And `aggregate_signature` is:

```
[ argmode ] [ argname ] argtype [ , ... ] |
[ [ argmode ] [ argname ] argtype : ,..] ] ORDER BY [ argmode ]
  [ argname ] argtype [ ,.. ]
```

 For more details we can refer to `http://www.postgresql.org/ docs/9.4/static/sql-alterextension.html`.

Let's describe the parameter used in the ALTER EXTENSION command:

- `Extension_name`: This is the name of an installed extension
- UPDATE: This will update the extension to a newer version
- SET SCHEMA: This will move the extension objects into another schema
- ADD `member_object`: This will add an existing object to the extension
- DROP `member_object`: This will remove a member object from the extension

 Only owners of the extension or a superuser can alter an extension.

- `new_version`: This gives the new version of the extension
- `new_schema`: This gives the new schema for the extension
- `object_name`, `aggregate_name`, `function_name`, and `operator_name`: These are the names of objects to be added to or removed from the extension

- `aggregate_type`: This is an input data type on which the aggregate functions operate
- `source_type` and `target_type`: These are the name of the source and target data types of the cast
- `argmode`: This is the mode of a function argument, that is, `IN`, `OUT`, `INOUT`, or `VARIADIC`. If omitted, the default mode is `IN`
- `argname`: This is the name of a function argument
- `argtype`: This is the data type(s) of the function's arguments
- `left_type`, `right_type`: These are the data type(s) of the operator's arguments
- `PROCEDURAL`: This is a noise word. Noise words are keywords/reserved words that are optional in the program and if not implemented, will still make the program run

Let's try to update the `adminpack` extension to version 2.0. using the following statement:

```
warehouse_db=# ALTER EXTENSION adminpack UPDATE TO '2.0';
```

You will get an error if your PostgreSQL's installation does not have 2.0 for `adminpack`.

If the user wants to change the schema of the `adminpack` extension to another schema and the `adminpack` extension supports `SET SCHEMA`, then the following command is used:

```
ALTER EXTENSION adminpack SET SCHEMA schema_name;
```

If the user wants to add an existing function to the `adminpack` extension, then using the following command can do it:

```
ALTER EXTENSION adminpack ADD FUNCTION
  function_name(anyelement, anytype);
```

Dropping extensions

To drop the extension, the user can use the following command:

```
DROP EXTENSION [IF EXISTS] extension_name [, ...]
  [ CASCADE | RESTRICT ]
```

The DROP EXTENSION command will remove the extension from the database. Dropping an extension will cause its component objects to be dropped as well. Keep in mind that for removing an extension, you must own the extension or you are logged in with the superuser. Let us go through all the parameters used in the DROP extension command:

- IF EXISTS: The DROP extension command will not throw an error if the extension does not exist; only a notice is issued in this case

- extension_name: This is the name of an installed extension

- CASCADE: Using CASCADE will automatically drop other objects which depend on the extension as well

- RESTRICT: It refuses to drop the extension if any other object depends on it

To remove the adminpack extension , we can use the following command:

```
warehouse_db=# DROP EXTENSION adminpack;
```

The preceding command will fail if any of the adminpack objects are in use in the database. Adding CASCADE in command will forcefully remove all dependent objects.

How to check available extensions

The PostgreSQL extension system provides a way to check all the available extensions of current installed system. It does not matter whether or not you have created the extension, it will list all the available extensions with its respective version numbers. The pg_available_extensions view has all the information about the extensions. To check for the available extension, we will use the following command:

```
warehouse_db=# SELECT name, version FROM
  pg_available_extension_versions;
       name          | version
---------------------+---------
 pageinspect         | 1.2
 tcn                 | 1.0
 pg_stat_statements  | 1.2
 adminpack           | 1.0
 pgrowlocks          | 1.1
 dict_int            | 1.0
 isn                 | 1.0
 mongo_fdw           | 1.0
 dict_xsyn           | 1.0
 fuzzystrmatch       | 1.0
 insert_username     | 1.0
 intagg              | 1.0
```

```
    ltree           | 1.0
    timetravel      | 1.0
    worker_spi      | 1.0
    pg_prewarm      | 1.0
    btree_gist      | 1.0
    test_shm_mq     | 1.0
    seg             | 1.0
    autoinc         | 1.0
    postgres_fdw    | 1.0
    chkpass         | 1.0
    pgcrypto        | 1.2
    mysql_fdw       | 1.0
    earthdistance   | 1.0
    moddatetime     | 1.0
    citext          | 1.0
    plpgsql         | 1.0
    pg_freespacemap | 1.0
    tablefunc       | 1.0
    dblink          | 1.1
    intarray        | 1.0
    pgstattuple     | 1.2
    pg_buffercache  | 1.1
    tsearch2        | 1.0
    lo              | 1.0
    hstore          | 1.3
    unaccent        | 1.0
    btree_gin       | 1.0
    pg_trgm         | 1.1
    refint          | 1.0
    cube            | 1.0
    test_parser     | 1.0
    file_fdw        | 1.0
    plperl          | 1.0
(44 rows)
```

Beside the list of the available extensions, we can retrieve the installed ones using the \dx command:

```
warehouse_db=# \dx
                List of installed extensions
    Name     |Version|   Schema    |         Description
-------------+-------+-------------+--------------------------------
  adminpack  |  1.0  | pg_catalog  | administrative functions for
             |       |             | PostgreSQL
```

```
 btree_gin  |  1.0  |  public      | support for indexing common data
            |       |              | types in GIN
 chkpass    |  1.0  |  public      | data type for auto-encrypted
            |       |              | passwords
 citext     |  1.0  |  public      | data type for case-insensitive
            |       |              | character strings
 cube       |  1.0  |  public      | data type for multidimensional
            |       |              | cubes
 plpgsql    |  1.0  |  pg_catalog  | PL/pgSQL procedural language
 (6 rows)
```

Additional supplied extensions

In the default installation of PostgreSQL, there are some other extensions available on the system and they can be created using the CREATE EXTENSION command.

Here is a complete list with some information about all available extensions. There are many extensions available and listing them here is out of the scope of this book, but you can get the list of all available extensions using these SQL commands:

```
warehouse_db=# SELECT name, comment FROM
   pg_available_extension_versions;
        name          |                   comment
----------------------+---------------------------------------------
 pageinspect          | inspect the contents of database pages at a
                      | low level
 tcn                  | triggered change notifications
 pg_stat_statements   | track execution statistics of all SQL
                      | statements executed
 adminpack            | administrative functions for PostgreSQL
 pgrowlocks           | show row-level locking information
 dict_int             | text search dictionary template for integers
 isn                  | data types for international product
                      | numbering standards
 mongo_fdw            | foreign data wrapper for MongoDB access
 dict_xsyn            | text search dictionary template for extended
                      | synonym processing
 fuzzystrmatch        | determine similarities and distance between
                      | strings
 insert_username      | functions for tracking who changed a table
 intagg               | integer aggregator and enumerator (obsolete)
 ltree                | data type for hierarchical tree-like
                      | structures
 timetravel           | functions for implementing time travel
 worker_spi           | sample background worker
```

pg_prewarm	prewarm relation data
btree_gist	support for indexing common data types in GiST
test_shm_mq	test code for shared memory message queues
seg	data type for representing line segments or floating-point intervals
autoinc	functions for auto incrementing fields
postgres_fdw	foreign-data wrapper for remote PostgreSQL servers
chkpass	data type for auto-encrypted passwords
pgcrypto	cryptographic functions
mysql_fdw	foreign data wrapper for querying a MySQL server
earthdistance	calculate great-circle distances on the surface of the Earth
moddatetime	functions for tracking last modification time
citext	data type for case-insensitive character strings
plpgsql	PL/pgSQL procedural language
pg_freespacemap	examine the free space map (FSM)
tablefunc	functions that manipulate whole tables, including crosstab
dblink	connect to other PostgreSQL databases from within a database
intarray	functions, operators, and index support for 1-D arrays of integers
pgstattuple	show tuple-level statistics
pg_buffercache	examine the shared buffer cache
tsearch2	compatibility package for pre-8.3 text search functions
lo	large Object maintenance
hstore	data type for storing sets of (key, value) pairs
unaccent	text search dictionary that removes accents
btree_gin	support for indexing common data types in GIN
pg_trgm	text similarity measurement and index searching based on trigrams
refint	functions for implementing referential integrity (obsolete)
cube	data type for multidimensional cubes
test_parser	example of a custom parser for full-text search
file_fdw	foreign-data wrapper for flat file access

Let's discuss some of these extensions one by one.

The adminpack extension

The adminpack extension provides support functions for pgAdmin and other administration and management tools. Most of the administration tools need to manipulate the files; hence, these functions facilitate that kind of utilities functionality. The syntax for the adminpack extension is as follows:

```
warehouse_db=# CREATE EXTENSION adminpack;
```

Let's discuss the different utility functionalities provided by the adminpack extension:

- pg_file_write: The pg_file_write function is used to create a new file or append an already existing file. This can be explained using the following example:

```
warehouse_db=# SELECT pg_file_write('foo.txt', 'Hello
            World', false);
 pg_file_write
---------------
            11
(1 row)
```

  $ cat /opt/PostgreSQL/9.4/data/foo.txt

  Hello World

- pg_file_rename: The pg_file_rename function is used to rename an existing file. This can be explained using the following example:

```
warehouse_db=# SELECT pg_file_rename('foo.txt', 'bar.txt');
 pg_file_rename
----------------
 t
(1 row)
```

  $ cat /opt/PostgreSQL/9.4/data/bar.txt

  Hello World

- pg_file_unlink: The page_file_unlink function is used to unlink (delete) an existing file. This can be explained using the following example:

```
warehouse_db=# SELECT pg_file_unlink('bar.txt');
 pg_file_unlink
----------------
 t
(1 row)
```

  $ cat /opt/PostgreSQL/9.4/data/bar.txt

```
cat: /opt/PostgreSQL/9.4/data/bar.txt: No such file or
  directory
```

- pg_file_length: The pg_file_lenght function is used to get the length of file. This can be explained using the following example, in which we need to recreate the file as we just removed before using the pg_file_length function:

```
warehouse_db=# SELECT pg_file_write('foo.txt', 'Hello
             World', false);
 pg_file_write
---------------
            11
(1 row)

warehouse_db=# SELECT pg_file_length('foo.txt');
 pg_file_length
----------------
            11
(1 row)
```

- pg_logdir_ls: The pg_logdir_ls function lists all files in a log directory
- pg_file_read: The user can read the data from the file by making use of the pg_file_read function
- pg_logfile_rotate: The user can rotate a log file using the pg_logfile_rotate function

The chkpass extension

This extension provides a new data type chkpass, which can be used to store encrypted data. Most of the time, we need to store the data in a database that cannot be read or stored or encrypted like passwords. Any values encrypted before saving into a column shows that the data type is chkpass and cannot be read in clear text. Its value can only be compared with string literals or non-encrypted values of the columns.

Creating the CHKPASS extension using the following statement:

```
warehouse_db=# CREATE EXTENSION CHKPASS;
```

Creating the foo table using the following statement:

```
warehouse_db=# CREATE TABLE foo (id INTEGER, username TEXT,
             password CHKPASS);
```

Inserting data into the `foo` table using the following statements:

```
warehouse_db=# INSERT INTO foo values(1, 'foo', 'pass');

warehouse_db=# INSERT INTO foo values(2, 'bar', 'passwd');
```

Using the SELECT statement in the `foo` table:

```
warehouse_db=# SELECT * FROM foo;
 id | username |    password
----+----------+----------------
  1 | foo      | :5METYeTF6VjvI
  2 | bar      | :n/2sTOY2rduYs
(2 rows)
```

Using the SELECT statement in the `foo` table where `pass` is the `password`:

```
warehouse_db=# SELECT * FROM foo WHERE password = 'pass';
 id | username |    password
----+----------+----------------
  1 | foo      | :5METYeTF6VjvI
(1 row)
```

The citext extension

The `citext` extension provides a case-insensitive character string type. Its value is first converted into lower case before comparing. We normally need to apply either the lower or upper function to perform a case-insensitive search.

Creating the `citext` extension using the following statement:

```
warehouse_db=# CREATE EXTENSION citext;
```

Creating the `foo_new` table using the following statement:

```
warehouse_db=# CREATE TABLE foo_new (id INTEGER, fname TEXT, lname
               CITEXT);
```

Inserting data into the foo_new table using the following statements:

```
warehouse_db=# INSERT INTO foo_new VALUES(1, 'foo', 'bar');
```

Using the SELECT statement in the foo_new table with fname as Foo:

```
warehouse_db=# SELECT * FROM foo_new WHERE fname = 'Foo';
 id | fname | lname
----+-------+-------
(0 row)
```

Using the SELECT statement in the foo_new table with the LOWER function of fname as foo:

```
warehouse_db=# SELECT * FROM foo_new WHERE LOWER(fname) =
                LOWER('foo');
 id | fname | lname
----+-------+-------
  1 | foo   | bar
(1 row)
```

Using the SELECT statement in the foo_new table with the LOWER function of fname as FOO:

```
warehouse_db=# SELECT * FROM foo_new WHERE LOWER(fname) =
                LOWER('FOO');
 id | fname | lname
----+-------+-------
  1 | foo   | bar
(1 row)
```

In case of a citext data type, we don't need to call the LOWER or UPPER function while doing a case-insensitive search.

Using the SELECT statement in the foo_new table with lname as bar:

```
warehouse_db=# SELECT * FROM foo_new WHERE lname = 'bar';
 id | fname | lname
----+-------+-------
  1 | foo   | bar
(1 row)
```

Using the SELECT statement in the foo_new table with lname as BAR:

```
warehouse_db=# SELECT * FROM foo_new WHERE lname = 'BAR';
 id | fname | lname
----+-------+-------
  1 | foo   | bar
(1 row)
```

 The citext data type is not as efficient as text.

The cube extension

This extension provides a `cube` data type for representing multidimensional cubes.

Let's discuss the various `cube` functions:

- `cube`: This creates a cube with specified dimensions. This can be explained using the following example:

```
warehouse_db=# SELECT cube(10,10);
 cube
------
 (10)
(1 row)
```

- `cube_dim`: This gets the dimension of the cube. This can be explained using the following example:

```
warehouse_db=# SELECT cube_dim(cube(5,5));
 cube_dim
----------
        1
(1 row)
```

- `cube_ll_coord`: This is used to get the nth coordinate value for the lower-left corner of cube. This can be explained using the following example:

```
warehouse_db=# SELECT cube_ll_coord(cube(5,5), 1);
 cube_ll_coord
---------------
             5
(1 row)
```

- `cube_ur_coord`: This gets the nth coordinate value for the upper-right corner of the cube. This can be explained using the following example:

```
warehouse_db=# SELECT cube_ur_coord(cube(5,5), 1);
 cube_ur_coord
---------------
             5
(1 row)
```

- `cube_is_point`: This is used to check whether the cube is a point. This can be explained using the following example:

```
warehouse_db=# SELECT cube_ur_coord (cube (5,5), 1);
 cube_ur_coord
---------------
             5
(1 row)
```

- `cube_distance`: This checks the distance between two cubes. This can be explained using the following example:

```
warehouse_db=# SELECT cube_distance(cube(5,5),
                 cube(10,10));
 cube_distance
---------------
             5
(1 row)
```

- `cube_subset`: This is used to makes a new cube from an existing cube. This can be explained using the following example:

```
warehouse_db=# SELECT cube_subset(cube(5,5), ARRAY[1,1]);
 cube_subset
-------------
     (5, 5)
(1 row)
```

- `cube_union`: This is used for the union of two cubes. This can be explained using the following example:

```
warehouse_db=# SELECT cube_union(cube(5,5), cube(10,10));
 cube_union
------------
   (5),(10)
(1 row)
```

- `cube_inter`: This is used for the intersection of two cubes. This can be explained using the following example:

```
warehouse_db=# SELECT cube_inter(cube(5,5), cube(10,10));
 cube_inter
------------
   (10),(5)
(1 row)
```

- `cube_enlarge`: This is used to increase the size of the cube. This can be explained using the following example:

```
warehouse_db=# SELECT cube_enlarge(cube(5,5), 5, 5);
                cube_enlarge
-------------------------------------
 (0, -5, -5, -5, -5),(10, 5, 5, 5, 5)
(1 row)
```

The dblink extension

The dblink extension is used to query external databases (PostgreSQL) from within the current database session.

 Almost the same functionally is available in PostgreSQL foreign data wrapper (postgres_fdw) which is a more standard compliant.

The file_fdw extension

It provides the file_fdw foreign data wrapper, which can be used to manipulate data files in the server's file system. We already discussed this extension in *Chapter 11, Foreign Data Wrapper*.

Other available extensions

There are quite a few extensions available, and discussing all of them here is out of the scope of this chapter. Interested readers can find some more extensions and information available on http://www.postgresql.org/docs/9.4/static/contrib.html.

Summary

In this chapter, we learned about the features of extension, and extension versions. We also learned about extension creation process as well as the process of altering and dropping an extension. We also learned how to check the available extensions and about additional supplied extensions, and in detail, we discussed the adminpack, chkpass, citext, and cube extensions.

Index

Thank you for buying
PostgreSQL Developer's Guide

About Packt Publishing

Packt, pronounced 'packed', published its first book, *Mastering phpMyAdmin for Effective MySQL Management*, in April 2004, and subsequently continued to specialize in publishing highly focused books on specific technologies and solutions.

Our books and publications share the experiences of your fellow IT professionals in adapting and customizing today's systems, applications, and frameworks. Our solution-based books give you the knowledge and power to customize the software and technologies you're using to get the job done. Packt books are more specific and less general than the IT books you have seen in the past. Our unique business model allows us to bring you more focused information, giving you more of what you need to know, and less of what you don't.

Packt is a modern yet unique publishing company that focuses on producing quality, cutting-edge books for communities of developers, administrators, and newbies alike. For more information, please visit our website at www.packtpub.com.

About Packt Open Source

In 2010, Packt launched two new brands, Packt Open Source and Packt Enterprise, in order to continue its focus on specialization. This book is part of the Packt Open Source brand, home to books published on software built around open source licenses, and offering information to anybody from advanced developers to budding web designers. The Open Source brand also runs Packt's Open Source Royalty Scheme, by which Packt gives a royalty to each open source project about whose software a book is sold.

Writing for Packt

We welcome all inquiries from people who are interested in authoring. Book proposals should be sent to author@packtpub.com. If your book idea is still at an early stage and you would like to discuss it first before writing a formal book proposal, then please contact us; one of our commissioning editors will get in touch with you.

We're not just looking for published authors; if you have strong technical skills but no writing experience, our experienced editors can help you develop a writing career, or simply get some additional reward for your expertise.

SQL Server 2014 Development Essentials

ISBN: 978-1-78217-255-0   Paperback: 214 pages

Design, implement, and deliver a successful database solution with Microsoft SQL Server 2014

1. Discover SQL Server 2014's new in-memory OLTP engine and performance-related improvements.

2. Explore the fundamentals of database planning and the Server Transact-SQL language syntax.

3. Gain hands-on experience with the use of scalar and table-valued functions, branching, and more advanced data structures.

PostGIS Cookbook

ISBN: 978-1-84951-866-6   Paperback: 484 pages

Over 80 task-based recipes to store, organize, manipulate, and analyze spatial data in a PostGIS database

1. Integrate PostGIS with web frameworks and implement OGC standards such as WMS and WFS using MapServer and GeoServer.

2. Convert 2D and 3D vector data, raster data, and routing data into usable forms.

3. Visualize data from the PostGIS database using a desktop GIS program such as QGIS and OpenJUMP.

Please check **www.PacktPub.com** for information on our titles

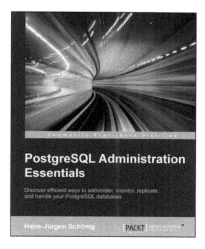

PostgreSQL Administration
Essentials

PostgreSQL Administration Essentials

Discover efficient ways to administer, monitor, replicate,
and handle your PostgreSQL databases

Hans-Jürgen Schönig   [PACKT]

PostgreSQL Administration Essentials

ISBN: 978-1-78398-898-3   Paperback: 142 pages

Discover efficient ways to administer, monitor,
replicate, and handle your PostgreSQL databases

1. Learn how to detect bottlenecks and make
   sure your database systems offer superior
   performance to your end users.

2. Replicate your databases to achieve full
   redundancy and create backups quickly
   and easily.

3. Optimize PostgreSQL configuration
   parameters and turn your database server into a
   high-performance machine capable of fulfilling
   your needs.

PostgreSQL Server Programming

Extend PostgreSQL and integrate the database layer into your
development framework

Henrik Krosing   Jim Mlodgenski
Kirk Roybal   [PACKT]

PostgreSQL Server Programming

ISBN: 978-1-84951-698-3   Paperback: 264 pages

Extend PostgreSQL and integrate the database layer
into your development framework

1. Understand the extension framework of
   PostgreSQL, and leverage it in ways that
   you haven't even invented yet.

2. Write functions, create your own data types,
   all in your favourite programming language.

3. Step-by-step tutorial with plenty of tips and
   tricks to kick-start server programming.

Please check **www.PacktPub.com** for information on our titles